FROM

START-UP

TO

STAR

KEN KUANG, JOYCE ZHANG, EILEEN HAN

FROM

START-UP

TO

STAR

20 SECRETS TO START-UP SUCCESS

Advantage®

Published by Advantage, Charleston, South Carolina.
Member of Advantage Media Group.

ADVANTAGE is a registered trademark and the Advantage colophon is a trademark of Advantage Media Group, Inc.

Printed in the United States of America.

ISBN: 978-1-59932-510-1
LCCN: 2014957789

Book design by Megan Elger.

This publication is designed to provide accurate and authoritative information in regard to the subject matter covered. It is sold with the understanding that the publisher is not engaged in rendering legal, accounting, or other professional services. If legal advice or other expert assistance is required, the services of a competent professional person should be sought.

Advantage Media Group is proud to be a part of the Tree Neutral® program. Tree Neutral offsets the number of trees consumed in the production and printing of this book by taking proactive steps such as planting trees in direct proportion to the number of trees used to print books. To learn more about Tree Neutral, please visit www.treeneutral.com. To learn more about Advantage's commitment to being a responsible steward of the environment, please visit www.advantagefamily.com/green

Advantage Media Group is a publisher of business, self-improvement, and professional development books and online learning. We help entrepreneurs, business leaders, and professionals share their Stories, Passion, and Knowledge to help others Learn & Grow. Do you have a manuscript or book idea that you would like us to consider for publishing? Please visit advantagefamily.com or call 1.866.775.1696.

To our Torrey Hills Technologies, LLC team members,
who made everything possible by working hard and smart!

— T A B L E   O F   C O N T E N T S —

FROM WOODEN SHACK TO WHITE HOUSE AWARDS CEREMONY

Ken Kuang's beginnings couldn't have been more modest. Born in rural China to a family of five children, Ken's first business experience was selling the fish his father caught to passersby on the roadside. Ken believed in the promise of America—that family connections and money weren't necessary to become a success if you were willing to work hard. He came to the United States as a Visiting Scholar to Clarkson University in 1994. His engineering acumen was matched by his entrepreneurial drive and, after his first start-up stuttered, he began the business for which he won the 2013 Tibbetts Award, presented to him at the White House, in which his company Torrey Hills Technologies was cited for Excellence in Small Business Innovation Research.

From its small beginnings, Torrey Hills has become a major player in supplying microelectronic components and process equipment, with an impressive 63 percent average annual growth rate and customers in more than 60 countries, and making the INC500|5000 list five times in a row, a striking accomplishment that's only one of many for this man who was born in a wooden shack.

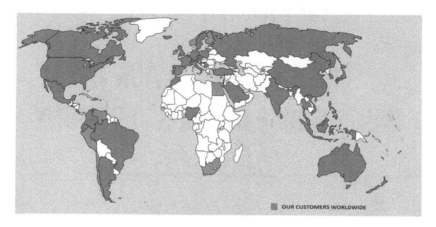

Customer Map

2013 Tibbets Award Ceremony in White House,
West Wing Auditorium

In this book, Ken and his colleagues Joyce Zhang and Eileen Han share their philosophies, insights, and the business savvy that has driven their small company to such amazing heights in such a short time. No matter what industry you're in, you'll find stimulating ideas, useful stratagems, and winning tactics that will help you grow your business from Start-up to Star Player, or to move your established business up to the next level of success.

Torrey Hills "Blue Chip" Customers

CREDIBILITY SELLS; HOW TO ESTABLISH YOURS

Establishing credibility is important for any business, especially when you are starting a new company, selling a new product, or building a new brand. Our experience in introducing a new product, the three roll mill, provides a good working example of how it's done successfully.

We started selling our Three Roll Mill in 2004. At the time, our brand was mostly unknown to the market. We were going against several established brands, all of which were very well known and well thought of. We had to work hard to sell our first 10 units, sometimes selling them at a huge discount just to persuade people to give them a try. Those who did give us a chance discovered that we delivered a good product and provided first-class service, and we received glowing reviews from those first customers. At the same time, and even with our limited financial means, we made an effort to give back to the community by creating a foundation to help underprivileged students. We put our nice reviews online, along with information about our efforts to give back to the community.

2013 Golden Bridge Award Winning T65 Three Roll Mill

After we effectively got the messages through, potential buyers saw that not only could our product be trusted, but also that our company could be trusted as a responsible corporate citizen. This gave us a huge boost in credibility; our business grew strong, and we began to receive inquiries from some of the most prestigious companies, universities, and research labs all over the world.

When those kinds of high-value potential buyers

> *Potential buyers saw that not only could our product be trusted, but also that our company could be trusted as a responsible corporate citizen.*

call, our salespeople make it their goal to turn them into satisfied customers at almost any cost, because with their positive endorsements boosting our credibility, we know we'll be able to sell our products to nearly anyone. Among these "blue chip" clients, we number HP, Boeing, Johnson & Johnson, CIA, NASA, and Godiva Chocolates. Having happy customers at that level makes it easy to convince prospective customers that our products will do a great job for them, too.

Strategy plays a big role in our day-to-day sales, including an approach we call "award marketing." Since 2008, our company has received many honors; some of these awards were given for our product, some to us as a company, and others for individual achievements. We have been an *Inc.* 500 or 5,000 company for five consecutive years. We have been one of the top 100 fastest growing private companies in San Diego for four years, and we were named San Diego's District Small Business Exporter of the Year in 2009. In 2012, our company was a finalist in the World Technology Award competition. Last year, we won a Golden Bridge Award for our product, the Three Roll Mill, as well as a Tibbetts Award for our research and development achievements. Why are these honors important marketing tools? It's one thing to tell the world

> *It's one thing to tell the world how great you are as a company, but it matters more when the message comes from someone with authority.*

how great you are as a company, but it matters more when the message comes from someone with authority.

As a team, we share the achievements and the pride; in fact, every team gets a duplicate of those award plaques, to remind us that we're the best in the industry. That assurance boosts the confidence with which we represent our company to potential clients. We know we're good, and we're proud of it.

As individuals, each salesperson comes from a different educational and cultural background. When establishing credibility in your field, it is important to recognize and deal with how you feel about yourself deep down, because the customer will sense and respond to any inner self-doubts. When you are an expert in a certain field, don't be shy about sharing your CV. Don't assume that a customer knows how qualified you are. Tell him your degrees, achievements, and how long you have been in your field. Don't expect him to do business with you just because you say you know your stuff.

For example, Torrey Hills President and CEO, Ken Kuang, has an engineering background and worked for Kyocera for a long time. When he's dealing with customers in the electronics industry, he explains, "I am an engineer by training. I have been an IMAPS member for over 10 years," so people are reassured that he is an expert and they're in good hands if they choose to do business with him.

Whatever your background, you need to be able to talk in detail about how your products work, and to tell your customer success stories. If your background is in sales or marketing, and you're in a technical field, you need to do the research and ask the right questions to be able to talk confidently with a customer. And that learning process needs to be continual.

Oftentimes in business, you run into people who badmouth their competitors; for us, that's not a winning strategy, and in fact, we go the extra mile to speak well of ours. Why? If I brag about myself, you'll look down on me. The flipside is, if I speak highly of a competitor, you'll think more of me and less of them. We once had a potential furnace customer tell us, "Part of your furnace is made in China, and I wouldn't want anything made in China."

Ken said, "If I were you, I wouldn't want anything made in China either." It took the wind out of the customer's sails, and gave Ken the opportunity to explain just how our furnace would do a great job for him. He made the sale by using a car analogy; a BMW is a great car, but a Toyota costs far less and will get you where you want to go just as reliably. Eventually, that customer made a purchase from us and was very satisfied with the quality of the furnace. By praising the competition, but by underlining our cost advantages, we got the sale.

> *If I speak highly of a competitor, you'll think more of me and less of them.*

We're often asked by potential buyers how our products compare to those of our competitors, and we always make a point of underlining our respect for their products—then go on to mention the awards that our product has won, mentioning the big-name clients who use ours if they're in comparable industries. Then we outline the technical specs of the product in question, making sure that the client knows it will do the job. The funny thing is, when we're praising our competitors, we find that potential clients will often offer up their own stories of how those competitors' products or service haven't lived up to their expectations—so they spare us from going negative!

How we view ourselves as individuals is important too, especially as many on our sales team are immigrants, because that means we're dealing with our own internal issues of feeling less than worthy; this is what's called the "immigrant mentality." When they start out, these team members often worry about their language skills and accents, and we work with each other to conquer those issues. But the basic principle is that they're representing our brand, which brings its own credibility, and that gives them the confidence boost they need to sell our products effectively. If you know your brand and believe in it, you'll communicate that to the customer.

SELLING IS ALL ABOUT THE CUSTOMER

Very often, your customers' needs are more complicated than just acquiring a product. Sometimes they need it fast; sometimes they need it customized. Sometimes the service is more important than the product itself. As a salesperson, you need to keep in mind that you're fulfilling a need, not just selling them a product.

Our company had a loyal customer who had bought many times from us, and they were happy with both products and services. But one day, they called us, very worried; they'd received a huge order that required an immediate delivery of two three roll mills to fulfill. We didn't have them in stock, and the normal lead time for an order of that scope is six to eight weeks. Their problem was our problem; how could we get them what they needed, fast?

While we were on the phone with them, we had a brainstorm; instead of trying to rush a production model while keeping them waiting, we could ship them two of our lab models immediately, so they could go into production on their order. At the same time, we could start production on two replacements. There was a hitch, though; we had just one demo model, which was in used condition, but the other one would be a brand new model. If we took it back to swap for a new one, we'd have to sell it as "used," at a discounted price. But considering their long-term value to us, we were willing to take that loss to ensure their continued loyalty. And it worked out better than we'd expected, since they ultimately decided to keep that new demo machine in addition to the two we built for them.

The lesson here is to put the customer's need foremost, and do whatever you can to fulfill that need, even if that means taking a loss up front. In this case, losing a couple of thousand dollars would have been painful, but worth it because that customer would become a customer for life.

> *Put the customer's need foremost, and do whatever you can to fulfill that need, even if that means taking a loss up front.*

Another illustrative story came from a pharmacy customer who had bought a mill from us previously. The mill worked great, but one day the operator accidentally dropped a spatula between the rollers. The rollers got stuck, the machine blew a fuse, and the mill stopped working. They were in the middle of fulfilling a big order, and when they called us, they were in a panic.

Now, even though this wasn't our fault, it was our problem. We needed to get them up and running quickly, because otherwise they'd lose money, and we'd potentially lose them as customers. The first thing we did was ship them the necessary replacement fuses overnight, without waiting for payment. Why? Because a happy customer is one you'll do business with again in the future, and a well-cared-for customer is a happy customer. We knew they'd be glad to buy from us again when it came to bigger ticket items, future machines, or parts that would cost thousands of dollars.

There was another pharmacy company who'd been using a smaller mill from another manufacturer. Their business was growing, and they needed a bigger mill. We sold them the mill, but subsequently they got in touch to say that they didn't see a lot of improvement in output. They were a local company and very close by, so we decided to drive to their facility and see what the story was. As it turned out, they hadn't set the correct gap size to get the maximum output from that machine. Instead of just adjusting the gap for them, we showed them how to find the best gap size and the optimal settings for the different types of ointments they were producing or might produce down the line. That gave them the skill set they needed to get the most out of the machine. We spent a lot of time on this education process, and left them very happy with both our machine and our service—and we charged them nothing for it. In fact, we wound up using this example as an online educational tool to help other customers learn to get the most output, and it was a real win/win for all involved.

> *Don't just look at the customer as someone you want to sell something to. Look beyond the sale to see their needs, and go the extra mile to fulfill them.*

The lesson here is, don't just look at the customer as someone you want to sell something to. Look beyond the sale to see their needs, and go the extra mile to fulfill them.

One of the cardinal rules of persuasion is that those whom we love will love us in return. Show the buyer you care; when the buyer likes you, he or she will be more likely to buy from you.

How do you show them you care, when establishing a relationship? Here's an example. When we're working with a company headquartered in a foreign country, we take a few minutes to research where they are. When a potential client from Turkey contacted us, the salesperson remarked, "Turkey is such a beautiful country with a wealth of historical sites, and it's on my short list of countries to visit someday." The next day, that person wrote back to her, saying, "Turkey is indeed a beautiful country, and we'd be happy to welcome you here." The barrier was down; she'd made a real person-to-person connection. We got their business.

It's important in this initial outreach effort that you be sincere, not smarmy. Other things you might comment on could include their product, their research, and their achievements. For professors, especially, people's appreciation of their research and what they do is very meaningful. That you've taken the time to delve into it is flattering, and shows that you care.

> *Before you field an inquiry, take some time and do your research on the person, the company, and the work they do.*

Before you field an inquiry, take some time and do your research on the person, the company, and the work they do. How big is their company, and whom do they serve? Have they been in the news lately, or received any special recognition? Having this kind of insight allows you to make the human contact before the business contact, and sets you apart in their eyes.

Have you heard of what's called the Ben Franklin effect in psychology? The gist of it is this: A person who has done someone a favor is more likely to do that person another favor than they would be if they had received a favor from that person. It's named after Franklin, because he described it as follows in his autobiography, where he talks about dealing with the hostility of a rival legislator:

> *Having heard that he had in his library a certain very scarce and curious book, I wrote a note to him expressing my desire of pursuing that book and requesting he would do me a favor of lending it to me for a few days. He sent it immediately, and I returned it in about a week with another note, expressing strongly my sense of favor. When we next met in the House, he spoke to me, which he had never done before, and with great civility. He ever after manifested a readiness to serve me on all occasions, so that we became great friends. Our friendship continued to his death.*

People make mistakes, and it is unavoidable that there are times when a customer isn't too happy with us because of problems with a product or with our service.

Ken, our CEO, once had to travel to a customer's facility to fix a problem. It is always awkward to communicate with unhappy customers. Most people's attitude is to get in, fix the problem, and get out; the less they have to deal face-to-face with the angry customer, the better. But Ken did just the opposite; instead of renting a car, he called the customer and asked him to get up very early and pick him up from the airport. The customer did—and in all their subsequent interactions that day, he was extra cordial to Ken, even introducing him as a friend to his colleagues. He never showed his annoyance, or complained about the disruption to his production; rather, he was warm and very accommodating to Ken.

Consequently, Ken spent a very comfortable day at the customer's facility. He fixed the problem, and everybody was happy.

> **It sometimes works in sales to ask a customer to do something for you; it's the Ben Franklin effect in action.**

This is an example of how it sometimes works in sales to ask a customer to do something for you; it's the Ben Franklin effect in action.

Another instance in which we've seen this effect at work is when we've requested samples of products made with our machinery from our customers: lipsticks, chocolates, or whatever they're making. They're always very happy to comply, because they're justifiably proud of their products, and our interest in them shows that we appreciate what they do.

It's also important to reach out personally to whomever you're dealing with, be it customer or colleague. For instance, we had a colleague back in our start-up days who felt underpaid and underappreciated. He took his complaints to a meeting with our CEO, intending to quit. The CEO listened first to what he had to say, then told him a little about his own early life, coming from a poor rural village in China, saying, "If it were 25 years ago, I would be a poor village boy, living in rural China. If you were to visit my home from a big city, like Beijing, and all I had were some chickens running around my shabby little village house, nevertheless, I would slaughter them and cook them to entertain my guest. Maybe to you, it would seem to be a very ordinary meal, but to me it would mean I'd given you everything I had to offer." He went on to explain that he wanted our employees to benefit, and to earn the kinds of salaries they deserved. Had the business been bigger and stronger at that point, this person could have been much better paid, but this was the best he could do in the situation. The person did quit, but he no longer felt that he'd been badly treated. In fact, they became great friends and are still working together on various projects.

Ken's son Simon did a science fair project on personalized medicine. Ken suggested than in addition to the data, theories, and graphs, he should personalize the presentation by talking about how these medications could be a breakthrough in the treatment of cancer—and how that related to his own family, in which one family member had recently died of cancer and a second was struggling with it. Many of the audience no doubt had stories like those in their own families, so they could relate—and Simon was named a Regional Finalist in the 2014 Google Science Fair and was one of 90 students chosen worldwide.

Joyce was working with a company that manufactures an ointment for the treatment of eczema, a fact she discovered as she was researching them ahead of their initial call. As it happened, her baby daughter had suffered from eczema, and she was able to say honestly how much she appreciated the work they were doing to relieve the condition, because of her child's experience. That bond of appreciation went a long way toward making the subsequent equipment sale and turning them into our customers.

QUESTIONS ARE ALWAYS WELCOME

In a technical field such as ours, our potential buyers naturally have a lot of questions. When customers have questions about our machines, we always begin our answers with, "That's a very good question," because by saying that, we let them know that their questions are welcome and we are very happy to answer them.

When customers come to us with detailed questions, it tells us that they are seriously interested in our machines and have actual need for them. We see in that expression of interest on their part that there is a real potential opportunity for a sale, so whenever a customer has questions, no matter how many questions they have, we make sure they know their questions are welcome.

By our willingness to answer all kinds of questions, we can also show them our expertise and let them know that we are good at what we do and we can do a great job for them. It's another way in which we can build our credibility. We can let the customer know that we have a lot of experience in a certain area, or that we have been supporting customers all over the world in a similar area with success, so they know they can trust both our products and our services.

> *By our willingness to answer all kinds of questions, we can also show them our expertise and let them know that we are good at what we do and we can do a great job for them.*

We also always try to anticipate other information the customer might want, and to supply it in our answers. For instance, if a customer, whose application we know is nanoscale particle dispersion, asks, "What is your smallest gap size between rollers?" we'd tell him, "For nanoscale particle dispersion, gap size is usually set around 20 microns, but you can adjust it close to zero," and mention, "According to the feedback from our customers, there won't be any agglomerate larger than five microns for your application." We not only show our expertise, but we also let them know we have experience in the area that's important to them.

Let's say a potential customer is interested in our three roll mill for TiO2 paste. We'd tell him, "We know Dye Sensitized Solar Cell very well and have shipped many machines to this field (including three roll mills and drying and firing furnaces). Specifically, you need to use a ceramic roller three roll mill for this application. We learned this from our customer 3G Solar in Israel."

Let's say that the customer's application is for nanomaterial dispersion, and he wants to know if our machine will work for that. We're able to tell him, "For your application specifically, many universities are using our products to process nanomaterials. Here is what Professor Such-and-such said about our machine," which is a way to share a good reference from another customer who's working in a similar area, ending with, "I'm sure we will do the same great job for you, too." We take every opportunity to show them we have experience and have customers in his area, and can give him great references from experts in his field. If he asks about references, we're always happy to give them, especially those "big name" references of whose work he's most likely to be aware. Knowing that these big companies or important researchers trust and use our machines makes it easier for him to trust us.

> *We take every opportunity to show them we have experience and have customers in his area, and can give him great references from experts in his field.*

One customer contacted Ken regarding his application for termination paste for MLCC or ceramic inductors. It just happened that Ken is very familiar with this kind of application, and was able to tell him, "I know the termination paste for MLCC or ceramic inductors very well. I spent many years making them in the 1990s and during my days with Kyocera," and included additional information about the machine's capacities and requirements that the customer hadn't thought to ask for.

We also hear from chocolate manufacturers who are interested in our three roll mill, and who ask if our machine is a good fit for them. We will answer, "Our machine is a great fit for the chocolate industry. Many chocolate manufacturers, including Godiva, bought our machines for their production and the product development process." We take the opportunity to let them know we have customers in a similar area and that they are happy with our machines.

If the question comes via e-mail, we add links to our websites where they can get more information, or links to our own videos showing our equipment in use. Because Ken has lots of experience in the thick film field, when we have customers in this field, we will always mention that we have an engineering team that knows the thick film technology and the three roll mill well: "With a combined experience of many years, you will get the top level of technical support from us." This reassures customers that our extensive experience in their particular area means that they can trust us.

By answering customers' questions, we can also let them know the great features of our machines. Sometimes, a customer who's comparing equipment from different suppliers will ask, "What is the advantage of your machine over the competitor's? Which model?" For example, a customer asked if our lab T65 model is any better than the competitor's similar model. Our answer was, "Our lab model has a higher throughput, up to 14 liters per hour, which is about twice that of the competitor's. It is a more economical choice if you expect growth and a scale-up in the near future." We give them additional information about the premium features that come standard with our machine, but which would cost them more if they wanted those premium features from our competitor. Sometimes, we add, "We have a fast response service team who always solve problems and keep spare parts on hand to our customers' specifications. Our engineering team will always be here to support you 24/7."

We've had customers who contact us with questions, and who mention that the competitor whose machines they're considering is located closer to their business. We respond in this way: "Although this competitor is closer to you, we offer first-class technical support 24/7." We'll also add that we have been supporting customers all over the country and internationally, and that they are all happy with our service and they've never found distance to be a problem.

Sometimes, a customer will ask us if we offer something out of the ordinary; for example, "Do you have the lease-to-own option, or do you have flexible payment options?" If we don't usually offer a particular plan they're asking for, we always do what we can to help the customer, because what the customer is really saying is he is very interested in our machine and wants to buy it, but may have a limited budget.

In one particular case, we had never offered a certain option before, but for this customer, since he was very interested and we wanted to win his company's business, we searched the Internet and found a car leasing company that offered a similar deal to the one he was requesting. We

> *If we don't usually offer a particular plan they're asking for, we always do what we can to help the customer, because what the customer is really saying is he is very interested in our machine and wants to buy it.*

came up with a contract based on theirs, with a similar payment schedule. When we offered this to the customer, we made sure that he understood that we'd done this exclusively for him. When the customer received this, he was happy and he placed the order right away.

After we answer whatever questions a customer might have, we'll always follow up by asking, "Did I answer your questions?" We will also be sure to add at the end of the conversation, "Do you have any other questions regarding our machine or our services?" or "Any other questions I can help you with at this moment?" We want to encourage the customer to ask more questions and to keep the customer engaged. By making sure they understand their questions are welcomed, we help them feel good about their decision to choose our products.

TIP #4

SEPARATE WANTS FROM NEEDS; UNDERSTAND THE STORY BEHIND THE QUESTION

Not every question is really what it may seem to be on the surface. Often, we find that a customer has a secondary question just below the one he's actually asking. For example, when he was looking at our smallest lab-size model, Mark, our client from NASA, asked, "What voltage is the unit? Is it a single phase or a three phase?" We realized as we heard this question that the actual question beneath this was his concern about what else they needed to do or buy to have their machine set up. We were able to tell him, "The machine is wired for 110 volts single phase. You can just plug into a regular wall outlet and start operation. We will include other accessories in the package and a few extra spare parts, too." Mark was happy, because we not only answered his question, but also addressed his underlying concerns.

We have a customer from the United Kingdom who was interested in a particular machine. It has two voltage options—

110 (for U.S. and some other North/South American countries) and 220 (for most other countries)—but, voltage in the UK is 240. Knowing this, when he asked, "What is the voltage of your machine?" we answered, "The voltage supply of our lab model is 220 volts single phase. We have shipped many 220-volt machines to the United Kingdom with the 10 percent fluctuation allowance and all of them have worked fine." That addressed his underlying concern.

Once, Phillips bought a lab model from us, one with stainless steel rollers. Before they placed the order, they asked, "Should we buy spare rollers?" When they asked this question, we understood that they were actually expressing concerns about the durability of the stainless steel rollers. We answered this way, "Generally speaking, the lifetime of stainless steel rollers is about five to ten years. It depends greatly on the hardness and abrasiveness of the material being processed. Stainless steel rollers can be resurfaced, so you will not need the spare rollers, at least for a few years. You can find a local machine shop to do the resurfacing, if needed." We got the order.

An Israeli manufacturer wanted to know if we had representatives in Israel. His underlying question expressed his real worry; would our support services be up to par for him, in that location? We told him, "We currently do not have a representative in Israel. However, we have sold machines to many Israeli customers, including Philips Medical and 3G Solar. They have been very happy with our products and services. Also, our machines are CE certified. We have a fast response team who solve problems and ship spare parts on time and to our customers' satisfaction, 24/7."

It's important when answering questions to separate wants and needs. Sometimes, our customers will want some features that we do not offer. When this happens, we will always try to ask the customer why they have such requirements, because sometimes we've found that what they think they want is not really what they need. Once we've established what they need, we can explain how they can achieve their goals using our machine, without the unnecessary features they're asking for. When we're asked questions like this, we don't challenge the customer's statements, and we make a point of respecting their egos and authority. The first response is always, "That's a great feature." We acknowledge their ideas first and then present our case.

> *It's important when answering questions to separate wants and needs.*

For instance, a lot of customers in pharmacy companies like the three roll mill machine with removable rollers. Sometimes, they ask, "Are your rollers removable?" But our rollers are not removable. We ask them why they need it, and they explain that they think it will make cleaning the machine easier. Once we know that's what they're after, we can present the case: "The rollers of our machine are not removable, but it's not necessary to remove them for cleaning purposes. We do not recommend the customers remove rollers by themselves, because you may need special tools and an engineering tech to do it. That said, these machines have the slow-speed wash-up mode, which is optimal for easy cleaning." Then we'll tell them about customers with needs similar to theirs who use our machines with success, and we share a link to an instructional YouTube video online to show them how to operate and clean our small lab-size model, and how to use the slow-speed wash-up mode.

Another example was a customer who was buying our three roll mill machine, but wanted to know if he could get it with two sets of rollers, both the stainless steel and the ceramic rollers. Most of our customers want only one set; if metal contamination is a concern, they just buy the ceramic rollers. If there is no metal contamination concern, then they simply use the stainless steel rollers. For these kinds of machines, it's not good to frequently change out the rollers, so we do not recommend that, but when a customer has such concerns, our first question is, "Why do you need two sets of rollers?"

The customer explained that although the metal contamination issue hadn't been a problem with the products he had been making, for his future research, the metal contamination might be a concern, so he wanted to have the two sets in case he discovered that he needed ceramic rollers. But as noted above, changing out the rollers isn't easy, and requires at minimum some special tools and an engineering background, so we don't recommend it. We assured him, "If metal contamination is a potential problem, you'll probably only need the ceramic rollers," and he ended up buying the lab model with the ceramic rollers.

Once, a customer needed some ceramic blades for our three roll mill machine. We did not offer the ceramic blades at that time, so we double-checked with them about why they wanted the ceramic blade, and got in touch with them, saying first that we had done the research on the availability of those blades per their request. Then, we let them know, "In theory, it is nice to have the blades made of the same material as the rollers," because they already had the ceramic roller machine. But in reality, ceramic blades wouldn't have achieved the best scraping efficiency. Over time, metal or Teflon blades will adjust themselves to match the shape of the roller perfectly, making sure everything on the roller can be scraped off neatly. Once they understood that, they were happy, because we'd understood that their real concern was the good scraping efficiency of the blade. They wound up buying from us and were happy with the Teflon blades.

ANTICIPATE CUSTOMER NEEDS, AND KEEP THE CONVERSATION OPEN

Being able to anticipate customers' needs means you can help them toward a sale without putting them in the position of asking for your help—and make a much smoother transaction for both parties. For instance, some of our customers have a limited budget within which they have to work. When we know this, we can anticipate that they might need some form of discount in order to put the price within their budgetary limits, so they can move forward. When that's the case, we can offer them some discount or flexible payment plan up front.

For example, we have a government customer who liked our machines, but they wouldn't move forward for a long time. We found out that their capital budget was $10,000. They were interested in our lab-size model, which has a listing price over that amount, so we had an in-house discussion about making the price easier for them to accept.

We couched the offer in these terms, "This model generally goes for more than $10,000. We really don't generally offer a deep discount for a popular model like this one, but for you, we will offer a one-time goodwill discount of such and such, which will bring the price down to under $10,000. We hope this helps if your capital budget is set at that figure, as most companies' are." After hearing this offer, they moved forward right away. We got ourselves another government customer, with the prospect of future purchases.

> *Being able to anticipate customers' needs means you can help them toward a sale without putting them in the position of asking for your help—and make a much smoother transaction for both parties.*

In another case, the customer was just a regular company; in our initial conversations, they mentioned that they had some capital budget restrictions. They didn't tell us what that number was, so we formulated our offer like this: "The basic model with the stainless steel rollers starts at $12,000, for example, and the ceramic one costs more. Most companies' capital budget starts at $10,000. If this is true in your company, too, let us have an internal discussion about how we could give you a discount to make it under that price point for you. Would that work for you?" At that point, they told us what their capital budget was, so we worked with them to give them a better price, and they moved forward.

Another customer told us that their capital budget was $5,000 and that anything higher than that had to go through an approval process that involved numerous departments and many people, and could take as long as three or four months. The machine they needed was priced at around $10,000. We asked them, "If we split the cost into two smaller orders, each order will be under $5,000. Will this work for you? This way, you don't have to go through the approval process and can have it sooner." That made it possible for them to move ahead and get their machine in a timely way. We've made variations of that offer—breaking an order into multiple orders to get it past the capital budget threshold—over the years, and it's helped a lot of our customers toward buying what they need.

In a case where we see that a customer isn't moving forward, we can also offer a flexible payment plan to meet their needs. This often makes it easier for them to go back to their management team and get them on board with their purchase. That's a win/win for everyone concerned.

Sometimes, the problem isn't money, but rather a lack of familiarity with our products. We had a customer who was interested in buying one of our mills; he liked the machine and the price was not a problem, but he had some uncertainty about the performance of our machines because he never used one before. Knowing he had those uncertainties, we offered him a lease-to-own option that would allow him to lease our machine for a few months. If he liked it, he could buy it outright: If he didn't like it, he could return it to us. The customer was very happy with the lease-to-own option, because it meant that he had the opportu-

> *Sometimes, the problem isn't money, but rather a lack of familiarity with our products.*

nity to try out the machine without investing too much money. He leased the machine and after two months, he bought it.

Giving the customer a win/win proposition is an important piece of sales success. We had a customer, a manufacturer of dental products, who was working with a limited budget, and offering him a small discount off the price wasn't going to be adequate. We tried offering him a flexible payment plan, but that offer was rejected too. Our team got together to discuss how we might move this customer forward and close the deal, and we came up with something new; if they were willing to provide an instructional video showing how they were using our lab model, showing it in use, or if they were willing to provide a testimonial to the lab model, we could afford to give them a hefty discount and would have those materials to use on our website for marketing purposes. When potential customers who might be in the same industry as this customer look at the videos or testimonial, they'd have confidence that the machine would work for them, too. This worked out very well, not only for this customer, but also for several others as well. A real win/win.

Another customer contacted us to say that payment wasn't a problem, but that they needed the machine he was ordering right away. We didn't have the machine, a small lab-sized model, in stock at that point, and the lead time for production was three to four weeks, which was a problem for this customer, who couldn't wait that long. We made him an offer that made everyone involved a winner: "We have a lab-model demo machine in our lab. If you need it urgently, you can use it for free until the new machine arrives." This offer was, of course, predicated on him placing an order with us within a month. That offer worked for him, and he placed the order that same day.

A similar situation came up with a pharmaceutical company, who had an immediate need for a large three roll mill, our 6-by-12-inch model. We didn't have one in stock, and the production time for such a big machine was six to 10 weeks. We didn't have the 6-by-12-inch model to lend to them, but we did have a smaller lab-size model. I asked him, "Do you think that you can use our lab-size model? If so, you can pick up the machine today to use and you can use it for free until the 6-by-12-inch model is ready." The customer agreed, because he'd approached other manufacturers and none of them had the larger model in stock. We were the only company that went the extra mile to try and solve the problem, and we were the ones who got his order.

When we're wrapping up a conversation with a buyer, we always make sure to ask a final question, because we want the customers to feel as though they're being well served and well informed, rather than rushed to a sale. Is there anything else we can do? Do they have any questions? Does the deal work for them? Give your customer a chance to express himself, and ask for what he needs without making him feel like he's being pushed toward the door.

> *Give your customer a chance to express himself, and ask for what he needs without making him feel like he's being pushed toward the door.*

Our sale cycle has several well-defined stages: qualification, sending out quotes, following up, closing the deal, and then after-sales follow-up. We receive a lot of inquiries from customers every day, but often we find they leave information out, so we always to try to ask more questions to be able to better serve them, to qualify if they have real needs or if our machine will be the right machine for them.

In the qualification stage, after we receive the new inquiry, we will ask what their application is to make sure that our machine is the right choice for them. If the customer didn't mention whether they want the small lab-size model or a big production model, we will ask, "What is your target throughput? If you let us know, we can recommend the right model for you."

We will also ask "How soon will you need the machine?" and, "Do you have a specific budget for it?" That makes it possible for us to get out ahead of planning for any special needs they may have. For planetary ball mills we will also ask, "Will stainless steel grinding media work for you? What kind of grinding media do you need?" Some customers have specific needs regarding the final particle size, so will ask if our machine will be good to get the particle size down to one micron or even smaller. Original particle size is an important factor to determine if our machine will be the right fit. Viscosity can also be an issue; we ask about that too, because we want to make sure that our product will satisfy their needs.

After the customer gets back to us with all the information, we will work on the quotations for them. When we're sending out our quotations, we will always ask at the end of the e-mail, "Does everything look okay to you? Do you have any questions we can help answer? Is there anything else we can help you with at this moment?" Again, this is to let them know that we welcome their questions and any opportunity to help them out. We always keep the conversation open and let the customer reply.

The next stage is follow-up. If we don't hear back from a customer within three to five days after sending out the quotes, we'll send an e-mail: "Hi. How are you doing? We just want to follow up with the quote we sent you last week. Does everything look okay? Is there anything else we can do to help you move forward?" Sometimes, we find that a customer would like to move forward, but has some impediment that he won't clarify if he's not asked. As long as the customer gets back to us, we will work to find a solution, and will create a proposal that best matches his needs. If he's got a limited budget, we can discuss used models, for instance; if he tells us when he needs to have a machine delivered, it lets us know whether or not this customer is ready to order.

> *As long as the customer gets back to us, we will work to find a solution, and will create a proposal that best matches his needs.*

Closing the deal comes next. If the customer asks us for a discount or for some other financial consideration, we're going to move to close by asking him to make a commitment to buy if we can provide the price he's requested: "Can you commit to an order if I ask my manager for that amount of discount?" If the customer says yes, then we will move forward, because we know that if we get that discount for him, he will place the order.

We can also ask, "Can you commit to an order if we waive the shipping cost for you?" If the customer says yes, then we have an internal discussion with management to move the order forward. When we offer a discount, we can give the customer the chance to commit by saying, "This offer will be good until the end of this month. Does that fit your budget timeframe?" That lets us know where they and we stand.

> **When we offer a discount, we can give the customer the chance to commit by saying, "This offer will be good until the end of this month. Does that fit your budget timeframe?" That lets us know where they and we stand.**

A week after the machine has shipped, we follow up with the customer; we do subsequent follow-ups in one-month, three-month, and six-month time periods. We will ask, "How does our lab model or production model work for you? Have you got any questions about the operation of the machine? Our engineering team is ready 24/7 to help you with any issues." The customer is always happy to receive our follow-up e-mails. Often, when we follow up with them, they express their satisfaction with our machines, and offer a testimonial. If so, we ask, "Would it be okay if we put what you had to say on our website for marketing purposes?" They usually readily agree to that.

Regarding trial closes, the same rules for asking questions at the end of a conversation apply to our distributors and the regional sales representatives or our partners. For example, we will ask our partners, "I just want to touch base with you and see whether your customer still has a need for a three roll mill. What will it take for your customer to move forward? We will do everything we can to help you win this deal." If we don't ask, we won't know why the customer wouldn't move forward, so we can't work with them effectively. We support our distributors and our district representatives in the same way, asking them what help they need from us to win an order. On one occasion, we followed up with them, saying, "Thanks again for offering our three roll mill to your clients. Please keep us posted once you get any updates from your customers. Our manager would like us to offer more support to you and your clients; if they aren't too far away, we'd like to send an engineer to stop by their facility to help them with the initial setup and also show them how to operate the machine." If we let them know about the benefits they can get if they let us know where the customer is located, they will tell us. Otherwise, some of our partners might not tell us, or they don't know and they didn't ask. We let them know that if they let us know, we can give support to them and we will also ask, "Do you have other customers who might need such machines in the near future?" If there are partnership opportunities between our two companies to build together, then we let them know that all our partners get a discounted price, faster shipment, and technical support.

> *We support our distributors and our district representatives in the same way, asking them what help they need from us to win an order.*

POSITIVE LEADING; HOW TO ASK THE RIGHT QUESTIONS TO GET SOMEONE'S HELP

The power of positive leading is what's sometimes required to persuade somebody to accept your suggestions, your ideas, or to help customers make a decision and to move things along. Sometimes, when you're asking somebody to do something they may potentially see as awkward or don't feel comfortable with, it's not good to frame your request as a direct question. Usually, you will get a negative answer—"No, I will not do it," or they may just ignore the question.

Let's say you ask a potential client, "Will you issue a purchase order?" If they're not ready, they'll say, "No," and you haven't gotten any useful information. A month later, you're still asking, "Will you issue a P.O.?" and they're probably just ignoring you. That's why asking the right question is key in order to know what the customers are thinking and to move things along.

Let's take, for example, our material mill test grinding program. Some people are not sure whether or not this type of equipment is right for them. They may have used other manufacturers' products in the past, and they are not sure whether our products will do the same great job for them, so we offer a special program: they can either ship their materials over to our office, or they can come directly to our office to use the demo machine to prepare their final sample. When they get the sample back in their facility, they can do their own tests, and then it's up to them to decide to whether or not to purchase from us.

It's a long process, and we were finding that people took a long time to act after the tests, sometimes not responding at all. We knew for a fact that wasn't due to a problem with the machines; they definitely get good results. We just needed to help them make a decision faster, so what we do now is ask some preliminary questions before the actual test grinding.

> **We just needed to help them make a decision faster.**

For example, we have a local customer here in San Diego who wanted to come over and use our demo machine to prepare his sample. The business had just moved; before that, they had rented a mill at another company's facility and prepared their samples several times a week. After they moved, they had to drive for quite some time in order to get to that facility, so it made more sense to purchase their own machine. The customer explained that he wanted to take the material to our lab and do tests.

Before making the actual appointment to set up the tests, we sent some questions to the customer, saying, "Since your time is precious, I would like to establish a mutual understanding. What would constitute a satisfactory performance for this machine? We certainly hope you would place an order after a successful test run. If you can achieve those results, then, theoretically, you should make a purchase from us."

The person replied, saying that, regarding our trial, it would probably only take 30 minutes, a maximum of one hour. "The resin mixture that we will try on the mill is an ingredient to one of our adhesive products. We will make a batch of our product using the material milled on the Torrey Hills mill and compare that to a control batch of the adhesive product that uses material milled from our current mill. We will then compare the control product to the product that uses a Torrey Hills Tech milled material." He went on to explain the specific criteria to be evaluated in the test.

We did the test run, and he took the material back. After a week, we called the guy and asked, "How was your analysis of the final sample prepared? Did our final product reach the standard that you had set earlier?" When he said that it did, we followed up with, "As per our agreement, since the machine has achieved what you have expected, it's time to issue a purchase order." It made things easier for us, and it made things easier for him, too, because it made it clear what he wanted. Within a week after the successful test run, he ordered from us and became a happy customer.

In another case, we had just signed a distributor for our ointment mill products. One day, he called and said, "I've got a potential

T50 Ointment Mill

customer, but before he commits, he wants Torrey Hills to fly us both to your San Diego office at company's expense." Now, we do want customers to visit us. We welcome them here to look at our manufacturing facility, to see how we work, and how our customer service department works for the customers. However, we can't afford to fly every potential customer to our facility. A healthy business can't afford to operate in this matter.

But instead of asking the distributor to tell him "No," we told him that we needed to know from this potential buyer when he needed the machine, how much of a budget he had, and other qualifying questions of that sort. Before these questions were answered, we couldn't be sure that that this guy was worth the expense of flying him out.

That let him know that we value his services and what he's done for our business.

The way we actually talked to the distributor also made a difference: "You are a very important distributor of ours. It is important that you can find as many customers as possible. We would love to fly you over to our facility at any time, at any cost, to have a look around and to have a drink with us." That let him know that we value his services and what he's done for our business. Then, we said, "However, we know your time is precious, and we want to you to have a high close rate. Could you please give this customer another call and find out when he needs the machine and how much money he has to spend on this machine before we actually spend time and money on this particular customer?"

Our distributor told us he understood our position, and was grateful for our invitation. He happily gave the customer a call on our behalf to ask the questions as we'd requested. It turned out this customer wanted to start a pharmacy, but he was not familiar with the business. He just wanted to fly out and see the equipment that was available. Knowing this, we were able to focus our energy on helping this customer understand the pharmacy compounding process and introducing him to all the equipment involved in this process, without paying for a trip. We helped the distributor to focus his energy, too. Positive leading made it possible to decline the request, yet make this person feel good at the time.

Positive leading is also important in closing deals, and harks back to what we discussed earlier, about learning what the customer really needs and asking the right questions to close the deal.

Some customers are straightforward. They ask for a close, they evaluate their options, and they make a decision according to their standard and the budget they have. Others are not so good at making decisions. They may have a limited budget, or perhaps they don't need the machine immediately, or they have a concern about whether our machine can do a great job for them. When a customer shows hesitance or does not respond to our phone calls or e-mails for a while, we call them up and ask, "We really,

> *You won't know that until you ask them, "What will it take for me to get your order?"*

really appreciate you contacting us for our product information, and we want to do a great job for you. What will it take to help us move forward?" Sometimes we'll make a joke and get them to laugh, which improves the exchange. Sometimes we find out that they need a bigger discount, or flexible payment options. But you won't know that until you ask them, "What will it take for me to get your order?"

It doesn't work every time, but sometimes it works, especially when you call the customer instead of writing e-mails. Sometimes they admit it's a money issue; that they have only $8,000 to spend and our machine costs $10,000. There are times when meeting our monthly sales goals mean that we need that $8,000, and we can offer him a $1,500 discount, but that doesn't come for free. For instance, we told one customer who was in this position, "If you could give us a short testimonial if you are satisfied with our product, or provide some pictures and videos of our machine running at your facility, we can give you this discount of $1,500. This offer is good for two weeks. Let us know." At that point, he came back with the $8,000 offer, and we closed on those terms. He felt great—he'd gotten the price he needed—and we felt great because we'd met our quota, gotten a testimonial, and sold our machine.

> **The bottom line is, don't ask if they're ready to order; instead, always ask what it will take for you to move forward?**

If the customer does not need the machine in a hurry, and they say, "It could happen in two months," then you might offer the customer a certain discount if he or she can place an order within a month. Sometimes that works, too. It gives the customer an incentive to act.

The bottom line is, don't ask if they're ready to order; instead, always ask *what it will take for you to move forward?* Sometimes the customer will open up and tell you exactly what he or she wants.

Clarity is important in positive leading. An illustrative example concerns the furnace product that we sell. It's a huge and complicated piece of equipment, and installation services are always required at the customer's facility. The customer has to test run the machine at their site before they give the final acceptance. Sometimes there will be a 10 percent payment not transferred to us before the final acceptance is done. We had a customer in California to whom we sold one of these furnaces. It's understandable that after the furnace was installed, he had a lot of questions, concerns, and requests for us—but in this case, they were neverending. No sooner would we do one thing for him than he'd have another request. Most probably, he was afraid that something might go wrong, so he wouldn't accept the furnace until the company was 100 percent certain of it. It took Ken asking him directly, "Could you please give me a complete list of things that we need to do before the furnace is accepted?" to get the customer to provide that list—and to agree that once those requests were fulfilled, he'd accept the furnace and make the payment. He and his colleagues made up a list with all the potential concerns and questions that they could think of, and sent it to us. One by one, we fulfilled their requests and answered their questions, and it was time to accept the furnace equipment.

Sometimes, we need to use similar tactics while asking a colleague for help. We had a customer who'd dropped a spatula into the feeding area of an ointment mill, and it stopped running. Our applications engineer suspected that the variable frequency drive was broken, but couldn't be sure. We didn't have a service center in that area, so our solution was to find a certified electrician who would contract to go to their facility, check on the machine, and help us change the variable frequency drive, if necessary. On a Monday, we told our applications engineer about the situation and asked, "How long would it take to have this accomplished?" He called around to contractors in that area and got back to us, saying that the machine could be fixed, and that the contractor could get out to look at it on Friday. But somehow the engineer forgot to send the replacement variable frequency driver to the customer's location, and also forgot to make the appointment to have the repair done by the contractor. That meant we'd wasted a week, and this was a good customer that we didn't want to lose.

Instead of asking him for an alternate date, we explained, "This is a great, great customer of ours. If you could help us solve this problem fast, you are helping us get more business from this customer. They need to have this machine up and running on Tuesday. Can you make it happen?" That way, we'd given him a deadline, rather than letting him define the time frame. Still, it didn't sound as though we were laying down a deadline. Rather, we were suggesting with positive leading, "If they need to have

> *You need to give some positive leading to the person from whom you want help for the greater good of the customer, and for the greater good of the company, and give them a well-defined goal to reach.*

this machine up and running on Tuesday, is there anything you could do to help?"

He actually called up more contractors around the area and tried everything he could to find a contractor who could go to the facility on the next Tuesday. He sent out the variable frequency drive overnight to the customer's facility. Everything was fixed on Tuesday. It was a huge success. The lesson here is that you need to give some positive leading to the person from whom you want help for the greater good of the customer, and for the greater good of the company, and give them a well-defined goal to reach.

Positive leading can work in a lot of ways. We have many employees who are not native-born Americans. Ken values his people highly, and when he thinks that a certain employee is a great value to our company, he will do anything he can to help the employee. When one of our best employees needed help getting her work visa extended and needed a green card, Ken was eager to help her out, even hiring a lawyer at his expense. However, because she wasn't an engineer but was on the marketing side, it was going to be harder to make the case that she couldn't be replaced. The attorney they consulted felt that her chances of getting a green card were slim, and didn't want to take the case. We had made the error of asking him directly, and had given him the chance to say "no."

> *Use positive leading so that you don't get "no" as an answer. Engage the person in the process of problem solving, and you'll get them on your team.*

A few days later, Ken contacted him again and asked, "Well, is there something that we can do to make the case? For example, if she published a science paper or if she receives an award from some organization?" That engaged the lawyer, and opened up his mind to finding ways that our employee could prove her value to the company and American society. He relented at that point and took the case, because Ken had asked the question in a way that compelled him to engage in finding a solution, rather than just saying "no."

Use positive leading so that you don't get "no" as an answer. Engage the person in the process of problem solving, and you'll get them on your team.

HOW NOT TO COMMUNICATE; THE GIFTS OF THE MAGI

A re you familiar with the classic short story, *The Gifts Of the Magi*, by O. Henry? The story is about the challenges faced by a loving but poor young married couple at Christmas. Each of them wants to buy the other a gift; she wants to get her husband a watch chain for his treasured watch, and he wants to buy his wife a pair of beautiful combs to hold her luxuriant hair. The twist ending is that the wife sells her hair to buy the watch chain, while the husband sells his watch to buy the combs. On Christmas morning, their gifts of love, useless as they both are, bring them closer together because of their mutual sacrifices. It's a touching story, but it also serves as a textbook illustration of how not to communicate, and of the dangers of acting on your own assumptions without being clear on what the other person wants or needs.

This kind of missed communication is all too common in business, and it's happened to us. For instance, we decided to surprise one particular customer with a free, unexpected upgrade on some features, and were stunned when the customer told us he wasn't happy. How could that be? The customer was in effect paying for silver, and we had given him gold!

It's not that the customer didn't like gold. The problem was our failure to communicate that we'd done what we did because we valued his business and wanted to show him that we cared. Had we started with good communication, he'd have been happy rather than put off.

In our personal experience, this kind of miscommunication is especially common with Asians, because we tend to be rather subtler. We don't generally express our feelings openly, even to those we love most. What works for us doesn't always work in the Western culture, and it's important to remember that.

A Belt Furnace Installed in a Customer's Facility

A Customer is Conducting Solar Cell Research using our Belt Furnace

We sold two large furnaces to a Wisconsin company that makes automotive components, a big company and a valued customer. When the customer reported that there were issues with the fans in those furnaces, we decided to send new ones free of charge to the customer right away. Now, our previous approach would have been to send a simple e-mail saying, "Neil, thank you very much for your e-mail. I am sending two fans to you today." But experience has shown that that gesture isn't always understood as the expression of care and loyalty that we want it to be, so the e-mail said, "Neil, you have always been an important customer to us. We want to make sure we go all the way to make you happy. We're sending two component spare parts to you free of charge because you are important," and we included the tracking number. The first piece of making this impactful was clearly expressing our love for the customer. The fact is that, even in technical industries, people buy based on emotional connections. We want the customer to feel our love, our care, not just the service. And it's important to be consistent in doing so, so that you don't wind up like the characters in the O. Henry story, disappointed by how your gifts are received. It's important to

> **The fact is that, even in technical industries, people buy based on emotional connections.**

61

know where your audience is coming from, and to try and see things through their eyes.

Have you heard about the book *The Battle Hymn of the Tiger Mom* by Amy Chua? The book is about her "tough love" approach to raising her daughters with the highest possible expectations, and how that worked in some ways and backfired in others. In essence, what she's trying to do is to communicate her love to her daughters—but she overdid it and spent too much energy being tough, and not enough communicating the underlying affection. What she was trying to tell them was, *I love you so much that I want to be sure that you to grow up able to survive and thrive against tough competition, so you need to study harder.* That's a way of communicating her love. But it wasn't a way that her daughters could really appreciate, and it made them angry and resentful of what they saw as impossible demands.

> **It's important to try and see things from the other person's perspective in communicating.**

It's important to try and see things from the other person's perspective in communicating. Take the story of a wife who'd stayed in bed all day because she felt ill. Her husband came home and, seeing that she was still sleeping, closed the door gently, went to the kitchen and started cleaning up and doing the chores. Instead of being pleased, the wife was hurt; why hadn't he taken the time to ask her how she was feeling? But her husband's point of view was, "You're not feeling well, so I thought I'd just quietly do your chores so that you'd get some extra sleep."

This is typical of miscommunication in marriage, and Ken has his own example. His wife was returning to the States after a visit to China, and he decided to meet her at the airport with a small bouquet of roses, thinking she'd appreciate the thoughtful gesture. She didn't; her first question was, "Why did you waste money on flowers?" Clearly, he had wasted the gesture (and the money!) because he didn't know what she really wanted.

These "crossed wires" communications can backfire in a lot of different ways. We were working with a big manufacturing company in upstate New York, and had just helped them to acquire and install a very expensive industrial furnace. An error in installation caused one of the key components, the muffle, to burn out, and we needed that part replaced right away. We wrote to our supplier, who responded quickly, asking for more information. We sent it; he wrote back with a quote, and more back and forth correspondence took place, ending with our placing an order and sending a money order. He started production; the piece was delivered. When you look at the interchange, he was responsive, and on top of the job every step of the way. He communicated well. But the challenge is that we had a factory of high-volume production shut down for about one month, and that month of lost of productivity is significant. How could he have serviced us better, and made us feel like a valued customer? How could he have shown us his love?

We have had customers who experienced similar problems. We handle them a little differently. First, we want to understand how severe the impact is on your production. If there's a problem that needs diagnosis, we'll check it right away—and the necessary component is delivered to you the next day, along with the technicians to install it. Our attitude is that we'll sort out the costs later, but the main thing is to get you up and running as fast as possible. We've been in business for 10 years, and we've never had a problem with a customer not paying. They're grateful for the service, and what it communicates to them; that they are valued and esteemed.

This kind of turnaround means that a problem can be solved in eight to 10 days, not a month, once we've determined what the problem is. Often, we ship the part without waiting for a money transfer or payment; once they confirm the part has arrived, our team is on its way. Shaving 20 days off the service time will save the customer a significant amount of money in lost production costs. The better you understand the customer's needs, the better you can communicate with and serve them.

> *They're grateful for the service, and what it communicates to them; that they are valued and esteemed.*

Cultural differences can have an impact on how we communicate, too, not only with our customers but with our foreign suppliers as well. We have an international business, shipping to about 60 different countries. We have a manufacturing plant located in Mainland China, as well as a supplier in Mexico. When we're explaining our corporate culture to new employees, we make sure they understand that their communications with the people at those locations have to take those differences into account. Because America has the reputation of being a powerful and rich country, many of those workers would be here if they could, and there's a tendency to feel like the "poor relation" when you're in that position. Thus, when we communicate to the factory, we must always be sensitive to our tone and careful not to sound at all condescending in either what we say or how it's expressed. Perhaps there's been a mistake made; of course, it has to be pointed out, but it's good policy to start that conversation with a compliment—something positive about how other work has been done, for example.

The best way is to ask questions, and lead them to discover for themselves that, somewhere along the line, a mistake was made. The straightforward way frequently backfires: saying, "What's going on with this shipment? You didn't send me this tracking number," leaves the person on the other end feeling as though your real message is that you make a lot more money than he does, and that you don't respect him as a colleague. Before you make any demands, take the time to consider how it will sound to the person you're addressing. Don't put that person on the defensive. At the end of the day, it's more important to focus on the results, not on your ego.

Previously, Ken worked for a big Japanese company that had a factory in Mexico. He'd visit once or twice a week, and he and his colleagues would always go out to lunch. They didn't think anything of it—the food was great, and by American standards a bargain, so paying for the lunch didn't seem like a big deal. But Ken began to notice that his Mexican colleagues were turning down his lunch invitations, making excuses about why they couldn't join him—and it dawned on him that those "cheap" lunches weren't so cheap on their much smaller salaries. They weren't comfortable with Ken picking up the bill, and they couldn't really afford to treat themselves.

For the same reasons, it was important to phrase any criticism of those engineers very diplomatically, so as not to give offense. It's too easy to come off like the arrogant rich American—even if you're Chinese. Otherwise, it turns into an exchange in which one side gets stuck on the defensive, and nothing is accomplished. Everybody's talking and nobody's listening.

> **Doing business internationally means you've got to be able to hear yourself as others hear you.**

The fact is, nearly everyone wants to come to America, because it's the number-one country, but because they cannot, they have very conflicted feelings about the United States. Doing business internationally means you've got to be able to hear yourself as others hear you.

NEGOTIATION BY PROXY

Negotiations between you and a potential customer are often not what they appear to be on the surface. Very often, the person with whom you are actually going to make the deal isn't even in the room—though, of course, you won't necessarily know that.

Once, a sales colleague was communicating via e-mail with an engineer in a company in San Diego. Ken looked at the distribution list, and knew right away that the actual decision maker was not that engineer, but rather one of the people who was being copied by him on the e-mail. He told our colleague, "Here is what is going to happen when you talk to the customer; you need to know who makes decisions and what his expectations are. And then you need to try to put yourself in the decision maker's shoes, and provide answers to his potential questions." As an engineer, Ken knew that the technical points had been satisfied for the engineer at the other end of the correspondence, but that that might not be sufficient to make things clear to the non-engineer vice president whose okay was needed to close the deal. The VP's angle would just be confused, and would likely have neither the time nor the patience to read the previous 25 e-mails we'd exchanged. Ken told our engineers, "Be careful on this one; when you are at the final stage and you're trying to close, make sure that you are also persuading the VP who sits in the office to approve this deal. You're not going to have a chance to meet with him or talk to him face-to-face. What he wants to know is that this machine will work, that it is being offered at the lowest cost, and will come in a timely manner. We need to make sure the engineer is happy—but also, when the VP reads this final proposal, he needs to be happy."

It's important, too, to be aware that a lot of things wind up being implied in communications after lengthy e-mail exchanges. Because you and the other engineer have been working closely on this for a long time, a long calculation evolves. In your final e-mail, make sure you summarize it clearly and concisely, so that when this e-mail gets forwarded to other engineers or the vice president, everything is clearly laid out on the first page, so they don't have to comb through the previous exchanges to understand the background or context. All the options should be laid out unambiguously.

> **Subtlety is key to negotiations by proxy. Doing your job properly makes your proxy's life a lot easier.**

Subtlety is key to negotiations by proxy. Doing your job properly makes your proxy's life a lot easier. And it makes the proxy's manager and superior's lives a lot easier too, in that they can rest assured that they're making an informed decision.

Consider a daycare center. You go to pick up

your child, you see that your child is crying, and you overhear the subsequent interchange between your child and her teacher. One of two scenarios plays out: Teacher A might say, "Why are you crying?" and the child says she's hungry. Teacher A offers her a piece of chocolate to quiet her. But Teacher B, in the same situation, takes the time to cut up an apple for her—a much healthier snack. Now, you're the parent—and at the end of the day, even though your child is the student, you're the actual customer, in that you pay the bills. Which of these interchanges is going to be more satisfactory to you? Your kid may prefer the chocolate—but chances are, you'll be far more appreciative of the choice and effort Teacher B makes, because it shows that she cares for your child's health.

It's important to identify who the customer really is in business, because they're our only sources of income. If I'm the parent, and I'm pleased with Teacher B, I'll be more than happy to spread this news to my circle of friends. "If you're looking for a preschool, I know a great one. This teacher is loving and caring, and she takes good care of the kids." I wouldn't have had the chance to ask Teacher A why she didn't do the same thing. Similarly, when we serve our customer's case, our engineer may or may not even have a chance to pitch our product and service to the customer and to the customer's VP. Therefore, we need to help our contacts/proxies to convince the decision makers.

Very often, in business, it works like this; the RFQ will come from a purchasing department. Again, since we're trying to pitch our products, we need to remember that it's a conduit. While I need to deal with the buyer's concerns about price and speed of delivery, it's also important for me to know who is going to be using our products, like our award-winning three roll mills, and how they are going to use them, because those are the people who will be making the decision. Typically, in a company, engineers in the background will make the decision. From an engineer's point of view, her primary interest is to get the job done in a timely manner, because that's what can put her neck on the line. It is the buyer's responsibility also to make sure the job is completed at the lowest possible cost. Likely the engineer will say, "I don't care about the cost. I need to make sure this project will get done." She's going to want to work with three potential suppliers, to make sure that the timeline is met.

Our first job is to convince whoever sent that RFQ that they can have confidence that we will do a good job. First, we need to establish our credibility with the buyer. The buyer is going to forward our quote to an engineer and say, "I got a quote on the copper tungsten flanges you have been looking for. What do you think?" Thus, in the first place, from the engineer's point of view, he's going to feel comfortable; "Hey, they know what they are doing." Without this confidence, price and delivery are all meaningless. When the buyer collects a whole bunch of quotes to send to engineering for approval, the buyer is going to forward this message to somebody. Somebody's going to take a look and say, "I'm going to work with this company because I feel comfortable. I know they can do a good job for me."

Look at the United Nations. A lot of negotiations go on in meetings in New York, but the fact is, the decisions are made back in the delegates' home countries, not on the floor of the UN. That's why you need to make sure that in your communications, you give the absent negotiators their due respect. Give them a lot of room. Give them a lot of the information. But also, make sure the deal you present is one that the leaders back on the home turf will find acceptable, because that's who your real audience is.

You're always talking to the person in the room as well as the person who is not in the room, and the one who's not in the room may hold all the power.

The buyer's job is to have a good, stable supplier, at the lowest cost. The engineer's job is to make sure, "I'm going to get a good product, and I'm going to get this project done." People in engineering rarely get involved in the cost.

> *That's why you need to make sure that in your communications, you give the absent negotiators their due respect. Give them a lot of room. Give them a lot of the information.*

Negotiation by proxy is a skill most of us use in our day-to-day lives without even thinking about it. Take the example of Ken and his wife; he flies a lot, and so has a lot of air miles available. Flying to and from Asia is a very long haul, sometimes as long as 13 to 14 hours. That can be exhausting, if you don't have space to lie down. Ken's in-laws live in China, and come to visit his family in California. Ken decided that a nice gift for his wife would be to upgrade the in-laws to a higher class fare, so they'd have room to be comfortable. While it didn't benefit him directly, it meant that his in-laws would have a better trip, and would talk him up to his wife—"Hey, your husband's really a thoughtful guy! What a great trip he gave us," which would please Ken's wife.

Establishing a warm relationship with a customer can have a positive impact on your bottom line in many areas. Take, for instance, the problem of timely payments, which most small businesses struggle with to some extent, particularly if your business is international. China's business side is infamous for delayed payment; it's bad. In the United States, typically, it's net 30, which means we ship and in 30 days we get a payment; on average, you're looking at net 45 to 60. Somehow, payment is always late, which is predictable. But the China side is much slower: Typically, you get net 120, or sometimes they pay in 180 days. Sometimes, this presents a significant challenge for a small company such as ours. Now, there's a culture of gift giving in China when you're doing business that's antithetical to American ideas. We don't participate in it, because it is against our business ethic. Second, the business is P&L, profit and loss, and this kind of thing is a P&L expense. If you give away cash, you can never make money. You can't even pay all the employees.

Establishing a warm relationship with a customer can have a positive impact on your bottom line in many areas.

But there are good ways in which you can build meaningful connections with your customers. Ken always extends himself to create a friendship with a client. For example, when he was visiting with a client recently, he noticed that the man's father, who was also in the meeting, would get up every half hour or so to go to the restroom. As you probably know, that's not atypical for older men, who often suffer this problem because of an enlarged prostate. As we've said, in some cultures it's acceptable to offer a gift to whomever you're negotiating with; in fact, it's expected. Not so here in the United States—but it's still good to show a valued customer in some subtle way that you care about him or her, and are thinking of them. You can do this in a sensitive way, that doesn't cross any ethical or legal lines or give offense. Ken had heard about a natural remedy, Saw Palmetto, and sent a bottle of it to the customer with a note saying he hoped it would help his father. In fact, it did—and the customer was really touched by Ken's thoughtfulness. So was the father, who told his son, "That Ken Kuang is a thoughtful guy!" That kind of support goes a long way, in business or in personal life.

Political life, too, is full of negotiation and communication by proxy. When the president or a presidential candidate gives a speech abroad, who is his real audience? It's the voter, watching him on television in the United States.

When we deliver important messages to our business partners or potential clients, we must be sure that we include all the information that is needed by the parties involved in the decision-making process—including those behind the scenes, who may well cast the deciding vote. Picture it like this: When you're discussing your quote with the buyer, you should be working side by side with your buyer to negotiate with the decision maker behind the scenes.

> *When you're discussing your quote with the buyer, you should be working side by side with your buyer to negotiate with the decision maker behind the scenes.*

PURCHASE DECISION-MAKING INVOLVES GETTING PAST A HIGH EMOTIONAL BARRIER

The biggest effort in making a sale comes at the point of decision; you've got to really aim for the fences.

As defined by Wikipedia, activation energy can be thought of as the height of the potential barrier (sometimes called the energy barrier). A simple analogy is a car's ignition system. When you start the car, it needs a lot of energy. There will be shaking or loud noise, but once it's started, it gets into the stable stage and only needs a little energy to keep it moving forward.

If we're working with customers to make a sale, everything is stable in the beginning where we're sending out quotes and they're responding. Once we're getting closer to closing the deal, sometimes they will have an emotional barrier that requires more energy to overcome; in other words, you hit a bump. That's what we mean when we say a high emotional barrier. But once they pass this barrier, they will get back to the stable stage and into their comfort zone, and everything will go smoothly. But first, we have to help the customer to get over the high emotional barrier. Once the customer is in their comfort zone, it will be easy for them to make a decision and move forward.

Have you noticed when you're signing contracts that if you're asked to simply initial here or there, you usually just speed through it—but when you're asked to put your signature on the line, you're far more likely to stop and read very carefully before signing? That's the emotional barrier kicking in.

> *First, we have to help the customer to get over the high emotional barrier. Once the customer is in their comfort zone, it will be easy for them to make a decision and move forward.*

Our CEO Ken is a great speaker but he hits an emotional barrier (feels nervous and has sweaty palms) just before he gets up on stage to give a speech, every time he speaks. Once he is on the stage and his speech is underway, he is back to being a great speaker again.

Our customers' orders are often over $100,000, and for some, it's much more than that. It's a very big investment and it's a big commitment, too, once they get our equipment in their facility. If it doesn't work, it will be hard for them to make any adjustments, and it's very hard to return such enormous machines. Installing them has already involved a lot of preparations and expense. Given these considerations, it's understandable that in making the choice to purchase such big and expensive equipment, our customers can hit an emotional barrier. Sometimes, if we ask too directly—"Can you approve this order?" or, "Are you ready to place the order?"—it will make the customer anxious, because all he can think about is the huge commitment he's about to make. But if we assume that the sale will be made and we ask intelligently in a way that helps the customer to bypass that barrier, we can help to make it easier for him to move forward.

For instance, we can ask, "Everything is good now. Can you confirm your requirements one more time?" We don't ask, "Can you approve this order?" because that's likely to trigger the emotional barrier. If we bypass that part and assume that the order is already a given, asking, "Do you have a loading dock that can be used for July delivery?" that doesn't happen. We don't ask them, "Do you want to place the order now?" We bypass that anxiety-provoking area by asking, "Do you want to plan for July delivery?" This helps the customer get to the stable stage. Another way of asking would be, "Can you fill out the customer form so we can get you into the system?" or, "When do you need the machine? We can start working with our factory now to make sure you can get it on time."

You can use this technique in your everyday life, too! A colleague who is married says that her husband doesn't like to undertake international travel—he hates the expense, and the inconvenience, which creates an emotional barrier to him saying "yes" to a trip. When she asks him, "Do you want to go to Italy in September or August?" it creates emotional barriers by making him think, "Is that when we should go? Which would be the better time?" Now, she simplifies it by making the decision for him: "Let's go to Italy next September. Where do you want to visit?" By asking this way, she helps him get over the high emotional barrier and gives him simpler options so it's easier to move forward. And she gets her trip to Italy!

OVERCOMING A SUPERIORITY COMPLEX

S alespeople are familiar with the "superiority complex"—or they should be. What is it? Here's a simple analogy. Say you're hiking in the woods and you come across a big bear. You're scared to death—but you know you can't show weakness or try to run, or you'll be in trouble. Instead, you stretch open your arms and make loud sounds to scare it away by showing the bear that you are superior, even though you're terrified.

A teenage son will often correct his father, loudly and sometimes even rudely. This is another example of the superiority complex. What he's really saying is, "Man, I want to be like my dad." What he thinks he's doing with all his corrections is showing that he's superior to his father, but deep down he's concealing that true sense of wanting to be more like his father.

We often see similar behavior with potential customers. Once, when Ken went to a customer's place of business, after a brief introduction, the customer said flatly, "I do not want to buy a furnace made in China." This is a display of superiority. What he was really saying was, "I really want to do business with you, but I'm going to beat you down first so I can get a good deal." Anyone who's gone shopping in a country where bargaining is the norm is familiar with this tactic: "You want how much for this piece of junk? Ha—I'll give you half that!" But deep down you really want it, or you wouldn't be standing there talking to the shopkeeper in the first place. A lot of salespeople in this situation feel discouraged, and wonder, "Man, what am I doing here?" But in fact, you're doing a great job. That customer actually wants to do business with you.

When Ken heard the remarks the customer had to make about Chinese products, his response was, "Actually, I agree with you. If I were you, I would never buy from China either." Then he stayed silent. The silence went on for maybe 30 or 40 seconds, a long, long silence, and got very uncomfortable. But Ken knew what he was doing; in effect, he was telling the guy, "You're bluffing." After all, this customer is a busy person, with a lot of work to do—yet he's taken the time to meet with Ken, knowing that Ken sells furnaces that are manufactured in China. Clearly, he sees the value. Otherwise, he wouldn't have bothered to reply to Ken's e-mails and phone calls, much less make a meeting.

Finally, it was the customer who broke the silence, saying, "Come on, I was joking. Let's sit down, tell me more." That gave Ken the opportunity to talk in depth about Chinese products, some of which are not so good—to agree again with the customer, before explaining why the furnaces we make and sell are great products and a great value. If someone is in a hurry to make a choice and doesn't know the product he's dealing with, he may well choose one built in the United States, because he's going to assume it's a better machine, even if it costs significantly more.

But if you have time to do a detailed qualification, and you have some budget limitations, you'll want to take a closer look at our products.

Ken went on to build up the company credibility, naming some of our best-known satisfied customers: NASA, Godiva, IBM, Apple—the kinds of names that give luster to our client roster. In the end, he made the sale.

It doesn't often happen that a new customer just jumps into your lap, saying, "Sell me your product!" Cold calling, in particular, can be quite discouraging; only about 5 percent of the people you contact will even get back to you, and the majority of those will be rejections. How do you avoid losing your motivation?

You need to think of the sales process as a continuum—like a piece of string. One end of the string is "strongly likes," the other is "strongly dislikes." In the middle is "indifferent."

> *Think of the sales process as a continuum—like a piece of string. One end of the string is "strongly likes," the other is "strongly dislikes." In the middle is "indifferent."*

Those people, the ones in the middle, will never be your customers. They're indifferent; they don't reply to your e-mails, they don't reply to your phone calls. They don't care. You will never be able to convert them. But your chances are much better with those at the opposing ends of the string, whether their initial reaction is "like" or "dislike." The superiority complex may lead them to seeming to be negative, even downright hostile, to your proposition. But the people on the "strongly dislike" end are willing to engage, because at the end of the day, they really do want to do business with you. When you pick up the string, the two ends meet. Somebody who really loves you will be your customer. And somebody who's thinking, "I will never buy a product from you," is also going to be your customer, because otherwise, he wouldn't have bothered to engage.

That goes too for customers who can get downright nasty with you, as discouraging as it is; "What, are you kidding me? That's crazy! I can get it for …" and so on. When the customer words it in such a nasty way, in reality, it's positive. This customer wants to engage, wants to negotiate, wants to communicate, and wants to talk. So keep the dialogue going, and you'll find a way to serve the customer and move forward.

Sometimes, you'll hit a bump with a regular customer—and sometimes it's a big bump, like a delay that will cost them some money. This could be a stressful moment for the team if they understand the consequence of missed delivery deadlines. Customers under this pressure may say something very emotional, because the stress is cracking their nerves. Knowing where that anger is really coming from makes it possible for you to simply reassure them, and to apply your calm to their fear. If a relationship is always perfect, it's never going to be a strong

> *Knowing where that anger is really coming from makes it possible for you to simply reassure them, and to apply your calm to their fear.*

relationship. Everybody makes mistakes—even we do. But our mistakes give us an opportunity to show the customer how much we're willing to do to make it right for them—and they won't forget that down the line.

Ken has a young son who likes remote-controlled helicopters. He bought him one online for $29, but when it arrived, it didn't fly. His wife was upset, and insisted she'd never buy from that company again. Ken wrote them an e-mail, saying he'd heard many good things about the company, but that this toy had arrived broken. The company quickly wrote back, asking for more information, which he provided. Then they sent him a new copter free of charge, telling Ken he could keep the old one for parts, and apologizing. That turned his wife's opinion of that company and its products around 180 degrees. But without that initial bad experience, she'd not have known how responsive and responsible they were.

Everybody's product is going to experience some problems; perhaps something is damaged in shipping, or it breaks after it arrives. It's the after service that really distinguishes your company from a less responsive one. Instead of arguing with a customer, hear them out and tell them you understand his situation. As long as your customer is engaged, the sale is moving ahead. If the customer is not engaging, it's indifference. That's when you're in trouble.

> *It's the after service that really distinguishes your company from a less responsive one.*

Once, a customer called with a problem first thing in the morning. "You're killing me!" she yelled. Everybody has those moments. You might want to say, "I just started my day; why do this to me?" But what she'd really just done was give us a chance to do a great job, to switch from super-negative dislike, to super-positive like. That's when your after service has to spring into action to make everything right as quickly as humanly possible. Once your customer sees how you're going to solve their big problem, they calm down. You just have to see where the negativity is coming from, and calmly counter their fears with the reassurance they're seeking.

A friend of Ken's, a business professor at a university, decided to quit his job there to start his own company. It was a risky thing to do. On his last day, a colleague with whom he'd had a cordial but casual relationship approached him to say, "What you're doing is stupid! You have tenure, and you're doing well. Why are you quitting?"

Most people would be furious and offended. Be careful about giving this type of feedback to your friends, because you could lose friends forever by talking like this. As might have been expected, Ken's professor friend was not happy, and he told Ken about the exchange.

But what Ken told his professor friend was, "He cares about you. You need to see beyond what he said to see the love behind it. He's on a mission; he sees his friend headed for what he fears is a train wreck, and he's trying to head it off."

> **When you see it from that angle, what initially sounded like a hateful speech is understandable, even touching, in the caring it shows beneath the surface.**

When you see it from that angle, what initially sounded like a hateful speech is understandable, even touching, in the caring it shows beneath the surface. Had he not cared, he'd simply have congratulated him and gone back to his business. The net result was a strengthened friendship between Ken's professor friend and his former colleague.

When you have a teenager in the family, you know that sometimes you have to speak harshly to them; this is how you demonstrate so-called "tough love." They don't like it; in fact, they resent it, and imagine that you're saying these things to be mean. But underneath that toughness is the love that says, "I want the best for you, and I'll fight anyone—even you!—to be sure that you get it." Once your child can see through the lens of your love, he or she will understand where you're coming from, and will be less likely to resent it.

We all have different ways of expressing our feelings, and very often we speak in anger when what we're looking for is reassurance, support, and understanding. Hearing the real message behind the words and tone can make you a better and more effective salesperson—not to mention a happier and more secure person.

> *Hearing the real message behind the words and tone can make you a better and more effective salesperson—not to mention a happier and more secure person.*

PRICE VERSUS VALUE

I n our business, we frequently enter into negotiations with our customers or distributors about price. There are three big pieces from our point of view that have to be part of every discussion and decision. The first piece is, what is the maximum revenue we can get from each unit we sell? The second is to be able to accurately estimate the volume we can sell. The third is to figure out the payment terms. Do not offer the final price until you find out these three important factors.

Price is certainly not the only thing a customer is looking for when they consider one of our products. There are other variables, the main one being its actual value to them. Sometimes, we simply cannot beat a competitor's price—which means it is that much more important to make certain

> *Regarding the value of product, what matters to our clients is the performance of our product, its quality, and its reliability throughout its lifespan.*

they're clear on the value of the product or the service we deliver to them.

Regarding the value of product, what matters to our clients is the performance of our product, its quality, and its reliability throughout its lifespan. The customer also needs to be sure that we'll be there to back it up with quick, reliable service. One of the ways you can show a new customer that you're worth what you charge is through the use of testimonials from past successes.

Let's say we have a customer who's considering one of our machines versus a competitor's version—and theirs is cheaper. How do we respond to a customer who wants to know why ours costs more? We let the customer know that while the competitor's model they mentioned or are considering does seem to be a cheaper and a more practical choice for now, there are other things to take into account when making a decision. We'll include some comparison charts between our model and the competitor's model for a reference. We let them know all of the differences there are in productivity and performance between the two models. We also will mention any awards that our model may have received, as well as its higher output, and greater power compared to the other one they're considering. Our model is also loaded with premium features, for instance, that the other doesn't have, and is more reliable.

Service, too, is a big part of our product; we have a separate service division that follows up on a regular basis to ensure our customers' continuing satisfaction, and moves fast to correct any problems. Can the competitor do the same?

We may not be able to match or undercut our competitor's price, but we will successfully sell the potential customer on these other aspects of our product; its quality, reliability, and service protection over the long term more than makes up for the short-term price difference.

Sometimes, getting the customer to really have a look at that overall picture is key to sales. At a recent trade show, we had the idea of sending out an offer of a free lottery ticket to potential clients ahead of the show, just for stopping by our display. The Super Lotto tickets cost $1 each, but visitors/potential customers had the chance to win up to $1 million. We reaped far more benefit than that small cost to us, in that many more people came to see us and take the time to look at our materials than would otherwise have done. We asked them to stay in touch and drop us a note about what they liked in what they'd seen, which reaped a lot of positive feedback and contacts. More to the point, it put us on their radar and gave them a good feeling about our company.

Giving something away—whether it's a lottery ticket or a good performance review, unasked, is a great way to build good will. For instance, we're a small company, but we use the services of a Fortune 500 Company, ADP, to do our payroll. Ken, our company CEO, was very happy with the attention and helpfulness he got from ADP's rep, so he took the time to sit down and write a glowing performance review of her work to her boss, the CEO of ADP.

> *Giving something away—whether it's a lottery ticket or a good performance review, unasked, is a great way to build good will.*

He said, "I want to commend you and your rep, Ms. Julia, for excellent customer service. You make the customers feel special.

While everyone has heard of ADP, I know that with such a large company it's generally hard to do impact tests since there are many customers. I'm the owner of a small business based in San Diego, with about 10 employees. We started working with ADP when Miss Julia converted my company over from our CPA, and she has been taking care of our payroll and insurance for many years. We know that in the scheme of things, we're a small customer, but Ms. Julia has never made us feel anything other than important. My staff and I would only contact her when we needed special support. Whenever we contacted her, she took the extra effort to make us feel special and valued. Please pass this letter to her manager in San Diego, and thank you."

Ken received an e-mail back from the CEO of ADP, thanking him for the letter—and Ms. Julia was very happy, because this was the first time she'd ever received a commendation e-mail from her CEO. It didn't take Ken long to write that e-mail, but we as a company will reap the benefits of it for a long while in terms of her goodwill and willingness to be extra helpful when we need her to be; a low cost to us, but a high value for all.

We often send customers extra blades they hadn't paid for or even requested, just to let them know we care and are thinking about their needs. We will also give some small parts or screws to our current customers when they need them. Sometimes, we will offer free shipping to our valued customers, even though they didn't ask for it. We will offer extra services, too, that are of value to the customer.

Much of our thinking on this comes from a book called *Influence, The Psychology of Persuasion* by Robert Cialdini. One of the key ideas he puts forth is the notion of reciprocity. In social psychology, this refers to responding to a positive action with another positive action, the rewarding action. As a social construct, reciprocity mean that, in response to friendly action, people are frequently much nicer and much more cooperative than predicated by the self-interest model. We find that our gestures of goodwill often lead to long-term relationships with customers, who remember these little extras and are more likely to do business with us in the future.

Often, we'll nominate a customer for, or recommend our customer apply for, an award that is suitable for them. Awards are a great way to let the world know about your value, your work, or your accomplishments, and add luster to your CV. We did this for a professor at UCSD with whom we'd worked on a project over a few years. We nominated him for an award, and he was very grateful and happy about it. It cost us nothing, but the value to him was high.

> *We find that our gestures of goodwill often lead to long-term relationships with customers, who remember these little extras and are more likely to do business with us in the future.*

LOWEST COST AND MAXIMUM PROFITABILITY CAN CO-EXIST

This tip is about how to serve your customer from a different direction. Many people see business as a zero-sum game; if I get more, you get less. As team members, our job is to make sure we provide excellent products and services to the customer, and at the lowest cost, so that our customers can be competitive in the market place. But, in the race to being the lowest priced, we can't give our products away for free—at least, not for long! That's where, especially from a business owner point of view, they get frustrated: "What

> *As team members, our job is to make sure we provide excellent products and services to the customer, and at the lowest cost, so that our customers can be competitive in the market place.*

are you trying to say? You can either have no cost, or good profit-ability. You cannot have both."

But you can have both; let me give you an example regarding IBM. IBM needed a furnace for their solar cell research. That furnace is one we'd normally sell for almost $90,000. Ordinarily, when the customer needs a furnace, we meet the need. The customer has a budget, and the customer is ready to buy—except that this customer had an extremely limited budget. But we need to make a living. If we sell a $90,000 furnace for $40,000 for a customer, the budget they had, we would lose a great deal of money.

Most people would give up, but not us. Ken knew they were ready to buy, but he needed to make a profit, and the amount they had to spend could not even cover the cost of manufacturing the furnace they needed. How could he turn a profit on that deal? He made the deal because he could see past the price to the marketing value of working with IBM, which was worth far more. He made them an offer they couldn't refuse: "My competitor would sell you this furnace for $120,000. I will sell it and install it for $40,000. And I guarantee I will do a great job for you. Everything's going to be ready to run, and it's going to be in perfect condition. Then, when you are happy, just allow me to use your name for marketing purposes. If you're not happy, you don't have to let me use your name."

How could they say no? Initially, we lost money on this deal—but IBM gave us permission to use their name, and that logo on our website was what sold multiple furnaces at more than double that cost, to customers all over the world, including Singapore Polytechnic University, UK Renewable Energy Center, Spain Instituto Tecnologico y de Energias Renovables S.A., ITER, and more. After all, it had worked for IBM! In the bigger picture, we were able to make a reasonable profit overall, and, at the same time, provided products to a very valuable customer at cost.

Another example was a Fortune 500 customer in Phoenix, Arizona. In effect, the customer had only a $2 budget for something that cost us $3 to make. This customer's item required special nickel and gold plating, because they were going to use it for gold tin brazing, a soldering process. Ken came up with a cost-cutting way to provide equipment that would do the job just as well, but using much-lower-cost immersion gold instead of the standard 2.5 micron minimum gold. He guaranteed that it would work— and it did. As we say in sales meetings, it's important to remember that when a customer comes to us trying to buy a drill bit, his real need is for the hole. Don't feel frustrated if you cannot sell the drill bit; you might still be able to help the customer make the hole, if you try it a different way.

It's important to remember that when a customer comes to us trying to buy a drill bit, his real need is for the hole.

Another customer came to us wanting to purchase our three roll mill, and specifically requested the ceramic rollers. These ceramic rollers are dense and strong, but manufacturing them is an expensive process, so they're priced higher than our steel rollers. When the customer heard the price, he was disappointed; it was beyond his budget. Even the offer of a discount couldn't put it within his reach. We asked him for more information; what exactly was he going to use it for? He told us he'd seen the machine on our website's opening page—and we realized that he hadn't gone further than that, and had assumed it was his only option. Once we knew what he wanted to do with the machine, we were able to sell him the stainless steel version, which met his needs perfectly and cost significantly less.

Very often, when somebody asks us to do something we cannot do, we assume the only solution is to throw money at the problem. If you have all the money in the whole world, it's easy to solve your problems. Lowering your prices to a level that prevents you from making a reasonable profit is just another way of throwing money at something. But in running a business, you'll go broke with this way of thinking. Try to solve the problem while still making money. Try to understand the customer and their needs—then find a way to meet them that will satisfy your need to make a small profit, too. It may require that you take a whole different tack in how you deliver or market your product. Just offering a discount won't necessarily solve the problem.

For instance, one of our colleagues had a child in preschool. The preschool offered a lunch for $5 a day. The kid tried it, but after a week of lunches said he didn't like them, so the family cancelled the lunch order. The lunch lady called to find out why, and offered the family a discount. They still said no—because the discount wouldn't make the child like the food any better than he did, so what

> **Lowest cost to the customer and the profitability can co-exist—but you cannot sacrifice one for the other. For a viable business, both need to be in the equation.**

was the point? A smarter approach would have been to reassess the lunch itself, and figure out what kids that age liked and would eat. Then, the parents would probably have been happy to pay an even higher price.

Lowest cost to the customer and the profitability can co-exist—but you cannot sacrifice one for the other. For a viable business, both need to be in the equation.

INSIST ON A WIN/WIN

nsisting on a win/win is a major point, and overlooking it is a mistake a lot of small business founders make, especially those with engineering backgrounds. They are somehow afraid of making a profit. They always make an assumption that you have to sacrifice to service customers. You have to spend money to solve problems, as we talked about previously. But as a business, you have to insist on win/wins.

> *Insisting on a win/win is a major point.*

Here's why: In our business, we have five key stakeholders: We have employees. We have customers. We have suppliers. We have our shareholders or owners. And we have the community. It's essential for us to build a win/win relationship with all of those five stakeholders at the same time. First, we have to make sure our employees are well and fairly paid, and have good benefits. Employees have to have an opportunity to grow. That's how we get and retain the best.

We are a small company. We're not able to pay big salaries like Google, Facebook, Apple, Qualcomm, or others on that scale—but we offer alternative value. From the employee's point of view, we will often exceed what a big company could offer. Our goal is to offer our employees the whole value package—to make sure that they feel valued, and that they have an opportunity to grow and to expand their reach into other areas of the company. Our smaller size actually means that the value they receive should be higher than the big company has to offer.

It's the same with our customers, suppliers, and all of our community. Where customers are concerned, you must always provide something that exceeds customer expectations. The value they get should always be more than they paid. The win/win in this relationship should be a value exchange, which is a different thing from the cost.

We don't want to do something where we would benefit but that jeopardizes the community. Often, we see manufacturing facilities that ignore this rule, to their detriment, especially in countries in which they're less stringently regulated than they are here in the United States, particularly in the area of pollution from chemical industries that produce a lot of exhaust and waste in water.

When we say win/win, we're talking about a value exchange, which is different from the cost or the money involved.

It's definitely happening a lot in China and Southeast Asia, where they routinely dump industrial waste into wild streams. This happened in the United States 40 or 50 years ago. These industrialists

INSIST ON A WIN/WIN

may see themselves as saving money—that's one side of a win. But the community is losing, and that's unacceptable.

When we say win/win, we're talking about a value exchange, which is different from the cost or the money involved. Here's an example: We have a piece of equipment that we would ordinarily sell for $11,000. Under what conditions might we be willing to give that away for nothing? Well, if President Obama said, "I need a three roll mill," we'd be more than happy to give one to the White House for free and send one of our engineers at our cost to go help set it up, because the potential marketing value of having such a customer would be far greater than $11,000.

Sometimes, hungry start-ups can be too greedy for the one-sided win: "Hey, we just started. We need to be aggressive." Sometimes, it is okay to lose. It's not always about the money. It's about, "I have a bright future." Find a way in which you and your customer can both win. And be creative—sometimes it's not easy. But if it's not a win/win, don't do it.

Ken has a phrase he likes to use to describe this; he calls it "the hungry goodwill." Deep down, if you're trying to look at the cultural differences between the West and East, especially on the China side, you could say it boils down to capitalism versus communism. Capitalism assumes everybody is

Capitalism assumes everybody is selfish. With communism, you're trying to promote a noble goal, a society in which everybody works for the greater good. But in reality, everybody is selfish.

selfish. With communism, you're trying to promote a noble goal, a society in which everybody works for the greater good. But in reality, everybody is selfish.

You'll probably have seen people in your own experience who get burned out from continually doing acts of good will, especially charity volunteers. They don't feel they're appreciated, and thus they feel frustrated because they're not getting the value return. People put a lot of personal equity into these efforts, but if the equation is one-sided, ultimately they quit. But the value doesn't have to cost money; this value could be an appreciation. It could be encouragement. It could be getting an award or recognition in a meeting; "This meeting was made possible from the numerous hours contributed by this individual." That's a kind of emotional payback that can go a long way.

We had a great sales rep in the USA. As a sales rep, he was paid on a percentage of commission; whenever he sold, he got a percentage. Sales reps make good livings, but sometimes commissions are up and down, based on the economy. This sales rep sold Company A $30,000 in goods. The economy had had a bit of a slowdown, but Company A is still doing really well with $10–$15 million annual sales. There's another company, B, very close to Company A, that uses the same kinds of parts. As it happened, Company A had a lot of stuff in excess inventory that they'd bought but hadn't used yet. So, the sales rep came up with a solution that worked for both companies; he helped Company A resell the parts they didn't need to Company B, even going so far as to facilitate a transaction that basically refunded the money to Company A, and also invoiced Company B. This was a good and thoughtful act—but once should have been enough, especially during a downturn, when his sales were very tight.

A good sales rep should do something like this. There's nothing wrong with helping out a customer—but he got nothing out of this exchange.

What he really needed to look for here was the win/win. If you are providing a goodwill service to friends, and you are not getting something in return, you may be okay with doing that a few times. Ultimately, though, there will come a point when the friend needs help again, and you're not going to be willing to step up because you're not getting anything out of it. You are basically volunteering, and that's not fair to you. If you let this kind of one-sided exchange go on for too long, you may even become bitter. And your friend will be surprised—what changed? You did, because you didn't look for your end of the win/win. Had the sales rep instead found a different product to meet the customer's needs, and identified what else he could help them with, he could potentially have either sold them something or facilitated a deal with another vendor, and collected a reasonable commission, rather than brokering their excess inventory without any recompense, all while wondering how to make a living in a down economy.

While you are helping friends, make sure your interest is covered. This is also important for family life. You see a lot of young moms get burned out; they get married, have kids, and all they're doing is giving, giving, giving and nobody takes care of Mom. It puts a lot of stress on the family, even when the husband is caring and wants to do his part. Those moms are missing the value part of the proposition, their share of the win. The value could be as simple as a heartfelt acknowledgement; flowers, a love letter, or praise. Maybe a weekend away from the kids would refresh her and give her a sense of how valued she is.

We all have goodwill. We have great hearts. But we need to take care of ourselves. You know what they say during those airline flight safety speeches? If the oxygen mask drops down, put on your own first before assisting others. That goes for business too, as in life. We serve our customers. We serve our stakeholders. At the same time, always keep in mind we have our own interests. If we're not getting something of value out of this cooperation, then we need to go back to the drawing board and rethink our priorities. Make sure that when we participate in something, our business interest can be taken care of too.

> *We all have goodwill. We have great hearts. But we need to take care of ourselves.*

Ken volunteers by organizing conferences for the International Microelectronics and Packaging Society, known as IMAPS. When people tell him, "Hey, you volunteer a lot. What is your secret?" he tells them, "Well, I'm selfish. I volunteer because I have a business. I only volunteer for those functions where I'm most likely to mingle with my potential customers. I have a chance to show those potential customers that I am an honorable guy, that I'm knowledgeable and trustworthy." That's a win/win for IMAPS, and for Ken. His business interests are nourished by his volunteerism, so his goodwill won't run dry. He also organizes Walks for Diabetes, for the American Diabetes Association, and is encouraging his high school-aged son to organize his own walk, not just to give back, but to have something meaningful to put on his high school applications. That way, it's a win/win.

Once we had a big customer in San Jose who was only willing to pay $1.20 for a product that we sold for $2. We needed to find a way to pull a win/win out—but how? This was a relationship we wanted to continue, so we had to find a way. First, we lowered our markup, and then we went to our manufacturing partner in China and showed them how to make this item faster and more cheaply, so their cost went down. It still wasn't enough to bridge the gap.

Then, Ken realized that the product we sold that customer was used with another product, which was sold by a company in Rhode Island. He went back to the customer, and said, "Can you talk to your supplier in Rhode Island, because if I cannot sell this product because of price/cost difference, he cannot sell his product either." If that company would agree to buy some of its components through our company, we could break even, even though we'd lose money in the initial deal with the San Jose customer. The customer proposed it, a deal was made, and everyone was happy.

The moral is, remember that your primary interest is to make a living, not to make a margin on a particular order. Look beyond the

> *The moral is, remember that your primary interest is to make a living, not to make a margin on a particular order. Look beyond the obvious and the individual deal, and find a way to make it work, insisting on a win/win for the long term.*

obvious and the individual deal, and find a way to make it work, insisting on a win/win for the long term.

CRISIS MANAGEMENT; HOW TO TURN CHALLENGES INTO OPPORTUNITIES

We all face all kinds of challenges in life and work. How we respond to those challenges can redefine the situation completely. As a business, we face many challenging customer problems. What keeps them from becoming crises is our commitment to top-class customer service—to making the customer happy, and to solving their problems. As we all know, retaining a customer is a lot cheaper than getting a new customer. Here are some of the things we always keep in mind when a customer comes to us with a crisis.

The first is, we respond in a timely fashion. We guarantee that we will address a customer's inquiries, problems, or service questions the same day.

> *We all face all kinds of challenges in life and work. How we respond to those challenges can redefine the situation completely.*

Second, if the customer is angry or confrontational, we don't take it personally, but recognize it for what it is; an indication of how stressed he or she is. It doesn't mean we won't do business with them again; when we solve their problem, they'll be twice as likely to come back to us in the future.

Sometimes, the problems are an outcome of an error by the customer—but it's still up to us to make it right. We mentioned earlier the case of one customer whose production line was halted when an employee dropped a spatula between the ceramic rollers of one of our machines. They couldn't afford to be without it for the weeks it would take to get it to us and get it repaired and returned. We offered instead to send them a new machine right away, and take the old one out for repair, so they wouldn't suffer that costly downtime. In our e-mail to them outlining this solution, we had to tell them that their warranty didn't cover operator damage such as this, and that the replacement rollers their machine required were costly. But to soften the blow, we offered them some discount off the list price of those rollers. They were delighted and relieved, and accepted our offer at once. As it turned out, they wound up buying the second machine as well as having the old one repaired, so it was a real win/win all around.

> **Sometimes, the problems are an outcome of an error by the customer—but it's still up to us to make it right.**

In another example, a small pharmaceutical company who'd bought a machine from us in the past now wanted to buy a larger production model, our 6-by-12-inch model. But when the customer received the machine, the customer wasn't happy, because the available power supply at his facility wasn't sufficient. We had confirmed the machine's power requirements with their buyer several times before the sale; since it's a production model, it's rated at 220 volts, whereas our smaller size model is 110 volts. And there was another problem; the larger model he'd ordered had to be partially disassembled in order to get it up the stairs to the second floor of his building, a problem he hadn't anticipated. They disassembled it, and managed to get it upstairs—but the machine wouldn't operate once they'd put it back together. The customer called us, angry and frustrated. We sent our engineer there the next day. He repaired the machine on site, helped them with the wiring, and gave them some training sessions on how to get the best performance out of it. The customer was delighted.

The engineer followed up with an e-mail: "Thank you for hosting me for the last several days. I really enjoyed working with you, and your team. They are very professional and detail oriented." He went on to detail the challenges presented by the difference in voltage, and how those problems had been solved. He explained that while they would be charged for the repairs and other technical hands-on work he'd performed, as a courtesy from our company they would not be charged for the extra day he'd stayed to train them how best to use the new machine. They were not charged for his traveling costs or per diem, and they were very happy with the outcome—so happy that they decided to keep a second, smaller model of the machine they'd planned to return to us, a loaner we'd sent them.

Wiring problems are often a challenge with larger, production-scaled machines when the buyers aren't sufficiently familiar with their requirements. Often, these are small businesses that are in the midst of scaling up to meet a heightened level of production. A customer who had just purchased a larger machine from us called us with questions about wiring, which were too involved to answer properly over the phone. We sent the customer the diagrams that were needed, but he still had questions. We recommended that he put a licensed engineer on the project, but he told us they didn't have one. This customer was located far away from us. Instead of sending our engineer there, which could take days and cost a lot more, we contracted with a local contractor to install the necessary wiring, and waived payment for the customer. All of this was accomplished within 24 hours, and the customer was very happy with the outcome.

Sometimes, our customers come to us with problems with older machines that they're having trouble with; sometimes, these aren't our machines to begin with, but they ask us for help in repairing them or replacing parts. Obviously, this is a challenge for us. How we respond is by asking the customer to consider trading it in. We will offer some discount on our new machine, so not only will they spend a lot less, they will get completely new machines that are trouble-free. We have used the trade-in program successfully many times.

> **We have used the trade-in program successfully many times.**

We had an e-mail from a customer in this kind of situation recently, asking if we could replace the worn-out rollers in his machine, and requesting a quote. We wrote back, "Thanks for your inquiry and your business. The cost of three replacement rollers for your model would be $3,600. Please allow us a couple of days to double check with factory about the availability and lead-time. Because of the age of the machine, those parts may no longer be available, but we'll check and get back to you." At the end of the e-mail, we mentioned that the latest model of the machine he currently owned had just won a prestigious engineering award, was a faster and more powerful machine that would increase his output significantly, and that we'd credit him a certain amount toward its purchase if he traded in his old one. Spelling out the advantages of the new machine for him made him very happy to trade up to the newer model.

We've seen this response time and time again; when we take the time and effort to make clear to the customer all they can gain in terms of productivity and ease of use by trading up and give them a proper discount, they see the benefits right away. We will always work with them to give them the best possible discount, warranty, and service, particularly if they are our valued customers already, and more often than not, they agree.

This trade-in program has been a big success for our customers and for us, because it's helped us to meet their challenges and offer them real solutions that work out to the benefit of all concerned.

> *When we take the time and effort to make clear to the customer all they can gain in terms of productivity and ease of use by trading up and give them a proper discount, they see the benefits right away.*

DISASTERS AND INNOVATION

In the history of the human race, many disasters have shaken up our world. Whether manmade or natural, we have had to learn from and to adapt to these changes and sudden events, and to look for ways to prevent similar tragedies from happening in the future. We call the process of implementing such changes innovation.

Entrepreneurs and inventors on the other side of history have always spotted market opportunities in even the worst disasters, coming up with innovative fixes to prevent human suffering in the future.

None of us can forget the tragic events in Newtown, Connecticut, in 2012 when a

> *Entrepreneurs and inventors on the other side of history have always spotted market opportunities in even the worst disasters, coming up with innovative fixes to prevent human suffering in the future.*

troubled young man fatally shot 20 children and six staff members at the local elementary school. This incident was not unique, unfortunately; there have been at least 74 shooting incidents on school campuses since this tragedy, 35 of them occurring on a college or university campus. The remaining 39 happened at K-12 schools. The rate of US school shootings since the Sandy Hook massacre averages out to approximately one incident every week, so parents and school administrators are all looking for ways to better protect their students.

One innovator created a product he called the BulletBlocker backpack. The cost is around $300, and the manufacturer claims to have sold an average of 100 of them a day. It is lightweight, and has a protective panel. The claim is that it can block bullets and protect the children from potential perpetrators. There are other products created for the same purpose, including the Bodyguard Blanket. Another product is the bulletproof classroom door. If a school has these bullet-resistant steel doors, teachers can just lock them and there is no danger of perpetrators shooting the door open and hurting the children inside. The cost is $1,500.

Another product is the bullet-proof whiteboard, priced at $400. Classroom staff can arm themselves with white boards that double as bulletproof barriers. The University of Maryland Eastern Shore purchased more than 200 of these whiteboards in 2013. The whiteboards strap onto a person's arm, enabling students and teachers wearing them to shield themselves from bullets.

Nobody wants to see a world in which products like this are called for—but here's a situation in which entrepreneurs have recognized a need created by a disaster, and designed products to mitigate future such disasters.

You probably remember the tragic explosion at the Upper Big Branch Mine in West Virginia that happened on April 5, 2010. It is estimated that annual economic loss due to coal mining accidents is over $45 billion worldwide. Although human error is frequently involved, these devastating incidents remind us of the highly risky nature of underground mining and the technical deficiencies in handling emergencies. According to the US Mine Safety and Health Administration, gas and dust explosion is the most significant single cause of coal mining fatalities. In coalmines, methane is a particularly prevalent cause of mine explosions. Torrey Hills team, Dr. Lai Qi and Ken Kuang, took inspiration from the coalmine explosion to come up with technology that allows the removal of explosive methane from mines. Our company filled this technological vacuum by developing a safe, portable, low-power, and standalone methane-capturing system that can be operated at ambient conditions and deployed underground.

A striking feature of this system is that it converts methane to methanol rather than oxidizing it into carbon dioxide. Methanol, the initial product of methane oxidation, is a desirable product of conversion because it retains much of the original energy of the methane while satisfying transportation and storage requirements. This project will deliver a technology that can effectively address all three methane-related concerns: safety, energy, and environment. The product can easily find applications in industries like coal mining, petroleum refineries, liquefied natural gas, chemical engineering, and EPA emergency response.

This technology won the federal Tibbetts Award and also a World Technology Award. We were finalists for an Oil and Gas Award last year. We are confident that this business will grow, create new jobs at our company, and will save many lives worldwide.

Let's turn to Jessica Lynch, the young American soldier whose gun was jammed by dust, a common problem in the Middle Eastern wars where dust is everywhere and machinery is constantly being fouled by it. Ken heard this story, and came up with the idea of a cleaning round that would cleanse weapons of this clogging dust. For example, the M16 rifle uses a magazine that has about thirty rounds. If the very last round, the thirtieth round, was a cleaning round designed to blast and create some pressured gas that can clean out the drum in seconds, then the cleaning of the gun could be done automatically without the shooter having to be concerned about the issue. Ken is still working on perfecting the design.

The threat of terrorism has been a tremendous spur to inventors, and a recent innovation in that field could well prevent a repeat of the Boston bombing. On April 15, 2013, bombs killed three people and injured more than 200 others when two pressure-cooker bombs exploded during the Boston Marathon. This brought home the difficulty of spotting potential terrorists in crowds, without disrupting everyday life. One company invented a very small, light, tri-mode, handheld system available for detecting trace amounts of explosives, chemical warfare agents, and toxic industrial chemicals. Another invention designed to spot terrorists at airports and depots scans the person's hands to check whether there is gunpowder residue or explosive residue on them. All of these innovations, born out of tragedy, have the potential to save untold lives.

Epidemic disease is another area in which we've seen disaster spark innovative brilliance. The SARS (Severe Acute Respiratory Syndrome) epidemic back in 2003 showed up first in Asia, then over the next few months spread to more than two dozen countries before it was contained. "Serial inventor" Horst Veith invented a product called SARS spray that stopped the virus cold. It has saved countless lives and contributed toward containing this terrible disease, was introduced to the air supplies of public transport and airports in China, and was widely distributed in South Korea.

Any disaster, no matter how horrifying, can be seen through the lens of innovation as a positive opportunity to do good and to prevent further calamities. The recent rash of heartbreaking news stories in which small children perished in hot cars when they were left inside is an example of a problem still waiting for a solution. The numbers are sobering; according to the Department of Geoscience and NBC News, a child dies from vehicular heat stroke every 10 days in the United States alone, and 73 percent of these children are under the age of two. An enterprising inventor will come up with a warning system capable of detecting a child in hot car that will sound an alarm to alert passersby. Perhaps it will even become a mandatory piece of safety equipment, like airbags. We can only hope it comes soon.

> *Do you look at disaster with the creative eye of an entrepreneur/inventor? You should. Every catastrophe contains the seed of an idea that can change the future.*

Do you look at disaster with the creative eye of an entrepreneur/inventor? You should. Every catastrophe contains the seed of an idea that can change the future.

———— T I P # 1 6 ————

MISTAKES AND INNOVATION

O f course, not every important innovation comes out of a disaster. Many of them occur by accident, or as the unlooked-for byproduct of an invention or medication that might otherwise have been deemed a failure and abandoned by its creators. The genius in this kind of innovation lies in looking beyond failure and envisioning a secondary application for your "ugly duckling."

Look around you; penicillin, microwave ovens, Coca Cola, Post-Its—even Viagra—all sprang from mistakes or failures, if you judge by what their creators had intended to accomplish. Ken had a personal experience with this kind of "innovation by error" when he was a manufacturing engineer with a company called Kyocera America. In

> *The genius in this kind of innovation lies in looking beyond failure and envisioning a secondary application for your "ugly duckling."*

one particular product, they would attach a piece of metal onto a piece of ceramic by brazing, a high-temperature process that takes place at 820 degrees C. Ken noticed some peculiar properties that the parts showed when they were cooling, and experimented with them out of curiosity, working with defective "reject" pieces. He dropped one of these defective pieces, expecting it to shatter—and was amazed when instead, it bounced. He didn't explore it further for some time, but after he left the company, he continued to experiment on it. What he found, when he bound the ceramic between two thin sheets of metal, was that he'd discovered, by accident, a process that made the ceramic shatter-proof, which meant it had the potential to revolutionize bullet-proof body armor used by the military. All of this culminated in a hearing organized by the National Academy of Science and Engineering at the Army Research lab in Aberdeen, MD whose members had heard through different channels about what he'd accomplished.

> ### *Anything put under compression stress will become stronger.*

Anything put under compression stress will become stronger. Standard ceramic armor can block a lot of bullets. But very often, soldiers get killed because a first shot will crack the armor, then the second shot will just go through. But with his proposed design, because the ceramic has a piece of metal on the top and bottom, the ceramic is super compressed, so the theoretical result was that, basically, it absorbs the kinetic energy and the ceramic will not shatter. Based on simulations, it will significantly increase the second shot survivability. Even the esteemed professors were amazed at this idea.

In science and engineering, we make a lot of mistakes. When you make a mistake, most people will feel bad. But we encourage our people to think differently about mistakes. If we make a mistake, it's okay; we all make mistakes. Calm down and think it through. You might have discovered something entirely new.

We manufacture a three roll mill. The rollers rotate to mix different materials, and they're supposed to rotate in one direction. Once, we were making a prototype for a customer in Houston. For this prototype, we needed a particular instrument to drive the rotating speed. This is called VFD—variable-frequency drive. We were working against a tight delivery deadline, and we had to make a tough choice to use a different sort of VFD than we usually did. The problem was that this VFD could also work in reverse, which they weren't supposed to do. But we had no choice, because this was Friday and the machine had to be ready on Monday. That Monday, in a meeting, Ken and Joyce realized that what they'd created by accident was a feature, not a bug. Why? Machine operators often get their cleaning cloths stuck in the rollers when the mill is running, and getting the

When we presented what otherwise would be a defect this way to the customer, it was suddenly a new feature and we were the only ones to have it—but remember, it started with a mistake.

cloths out of the rollers is a time-consuming process. Now, they explained to the customer, they had solved that problem. If you get something stuck, with the touch of a button you can reverse the roller direction and get it out. It also made the cleaning process much easier.

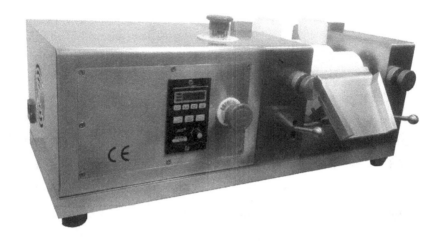

T65A Three Roll Mill

When we presented what otherwise would be a defect this way to the customer, it was suddenly a new feature and we were the only ones to have it—but remember, it started with a mistake that happened because we were in a rush to deliver this piece of equipment.

One of the world's most popular drugs—Viagra—was initially formulated to lower blood pressure. It didn't work for that, but the men who were testing it told the developers that they didn't want to give it back, and in fact, could they get more? The people who lose out in these situations are those who see mistakes as failures and who simply give up. Success is for those who take a second look from a different perspective.

BUILDING A WINNING TEAM

What is a winning team? In our company, we believe that the most important part of creating a winning team is that your team members like what they do. They feel comfortable with their daily tasks and enjoy their time at work. Their education and expertise match their job descriptions and their responsibilities. They also have great mentors and receive constant on-the-job training to encourage growth.

A winning team's members are motivated to achieve higher goals. They welcome challenges and take satisfaction in conquering them. They're self-directed and not afraid to make decisions. They are results oriented and actively pursue solutions.

> *In our company, we believe that the most important part of creating a winning team is that your team members like what they do.*

They seek personal improvement, too, and are aware of areas in which they need to pursue it. The company is behind them in this, paying for their education. They're appropriately rewarded for their achievements, via praise and monetary rewards.

What are our principles for creating a winning team? Ken has always felt that the most important thing managers can do is to be generous with praise and positive feedback from day one. When an employee accomplishes something special, make sure that everyone hears about it. For example, we were in the process of developing a new mill that had some problems with materials leaking off the roller sides. One of our engineers really dug in and worked hard at solving the problem, trying many different approaches. Finally, he developed a mechanism that allowed the end plates holding the rollers to self-adjust and prevent the material from leaking off the rollers.

We were all there for the final successful test, and everyone was very excited, including Ken. But the engineer himself was very quiet and calm. Ken praised him in front of everyone for solving the problem so creatively, and after the meeting he told him that it was great success, and that he should be very proud of himself, because he's a great engineer and had accomplished something very important. That talk from Ken really helped that engineer's self-confidence, because it made him see himself from a different angle. He hadn't just finished a job; he'd really proved himself.

Another example that comes to mind was when we were doing sample testing for one of our customers, a French chocolate maker. They wanted us to create a mill that would grind chocolate nut paste to a particular consistency, but it was a very challenging task, because the paste is quite thick and it required a lot of trials and measuring in order to find the perfect settings. It was a Friday, and two of us were there until 6:30, trying different settings, when finally we hit on the perfect way to process the material quickly and to get the right dispersion results.

When we were ready to leave, Ken was still at the office, and when he learned about our success in finding a perfect solution for the customer, he was excited. Because it was Friday, and he thought that we had made a tremendous effort, he went to his office and grabbed two bottles of wine, one for each of us. It was a very nice feeling—not just because of the wine, of course, but because his response showed us how valued we were, and made us eager to tackle the next challenge.

Positive feedback is necessary when you want to encourage an employee to take on a challenge. When Joyce took over sales, she was initially worried because she hadn't done sales in the past, and was afraid she'd let the company down. Ken encouraged her, saying, "You have always been a good communicator. You always have great ideas. You're a fast learner."

> ## *Positive feedback is necessary.*

He didn't think that there was any problem, or that she couldn't pick things up quickly and improve things considerably. That built her confidence, and after her first two months, sales really picked up. A big test came when the company received an inquiry for our products from the CIA. Joyce was a little shaky; we were still a relatively new and small company, and this was an important client. Ken told her, "Go get them. No problem. It's yours." That boosted her spirits, and made her want to prove him right in believing in her. She aggressively contacted the CIA's purchasing agents, and within two weeks had successfully solicited their orders.

It's easy to praise someone who's had a success, but it's also important to remember that praise, boosting confidence, and positive feedback are also very useful when an employee has made a mistake or didn't make any progress in his job. In another sale, Joyce was processing her first letters of credit from an Indian company, and although she did her best to make sure that they were in good order, she missed a key point. The letter of their request said, "No transshipment," which meant that we had to fly the machine from Los Angeles to India directly, without stopping at another airport. She didn't catch that wording in the terms until after we shipped the machine. She was horrified; would her mistake cost the company money, or cost her her job? What if the Indian company refused to pay?

> *It's easy to praise someone who's had a success, but it's also important to remember that praise, boosting confidence, and positive feedback are also very useful when an employee has made a mistake or didn't make any progress in his job.*

She went to Ken, ready to be fired, or at the very least severely scolded for not having looked at things more carefully beforehand. Instead, he shrugged. "Oh, no problem at all. Most people are good people, and they'll understand an honest mistake. You have done a good job all along.

Everybody makes mistakes and this is your first one, so don't worry about it. I've done letters of credit before and I've made mistakes before, but next time you won't, so no worries. Let's contact the customer, let them know the situation, and we'll revise the terms so that we can be paid." Joyce was hugely relieved, and when she contacted the customer, they e-mailed back that it was okay, and they'd go ahead and pay as agreed. By giving Joyce positive feedback about her past performance, and sharing his personal experience with having made similar mistakes before, Ken made her felt better about herself, and made it possible for her to approach the client confidently and resolve the problem.

Make sure a good mentor is available for every new employee. This mentor should be experienced at what he does and willing and able to communicate his experience to the new employee. Training materials are also important; we have great guidelines in place, for example, for our sales staff that allows even a very new salesperson to follow the right procedures.

> *Make sure a good mentor is available for every new employee.*

A good mentor welcomes questions and gives directions and beyond. We have a weekly sales meeting and questions are always welcome; we discuss the questions as case studies. We work together exchanging ideas for reaching out to our current and potential new customers more effectively.

Another important principle of team building is to be ready to adjust responsibilities when current ones don't work out for an employee. Sometimes, a certain job function just isn't a good fit. This is a good employee; he works hard, but he is not making good progress. The solution is not to fire the person, but to find a position in the company that will make better use of his capabilities and education.

For example, we have a colleague who came from Hong Kong, and when he chose to go back to Hong Kong to get married, Ken thought that since he was a really good employee, he'd like to give him an opportunity to stay with the company. He thought it would be a great idea if John could work in Hong Kong and become a regional sales rep for Torrey Hills in the Southeast Asian countries. John agreed to take the job—but it turned out he was good at fixing machines, testing machines, and developing new machines, but not so good at working with people and selling stuff. He was terribly worried that he wasn't making much headway in the region, and it became increasingly obvious that we had to make a change. Either we had to let him go or we could find him another function in the company.

As we've mentioned, we also sell furnaces, which is a type of product that tends to require a lot of hands-on work. When a customer buys a new furnace, engineers need to go to their facility to install the equipment. John has a Hong Kong passport, which is a great advantage because it means that in a lot of countries, he does not need a visa. Ken switched his job function to furnace installation and maintenance, and subsequently John traveled around the world to work with customers, installing and testing the machines. When customers had a problem with a furnace, he would go to their facilities to make the repairs. He had started out being a less-than-facile communicator, with less-than-stellar people skills, but in the new position he gained self-confidence and poise, and eventually became quite adept at working with people. After a while, he actually took over some of the sales work, too, so it all worked out.

The fourth principle is to encourage and support employees to receive further training in areas they are interested in. On-the-job training is part of helping employees advance in the company. Another way is to receive education from a third party. Our company always encourages employees to find such opportunities; for example, our office manager wanted more formal training in human resource management, so our company supported her and sent her to a weeklong program focused on HR.

> *On-the-job training is part of helping employees advance in the company.*

In the sales department, we order educational DVDs on sales, marketing, and technology, and have employee meetings at which we study the programs together. Our company also buys multiple copies of useful books to distribute inside the company, to encourage employees to learn new ideas and technologies.

Another important team building point is to motivate people by reducing their workload. That may sound counter-intuitive, but it works for us. In our company, when you are extremely experienced and good at a certain task, it's time to move on, to delegate and seek out your next higher-level challenges. That's how to achieve your highest personal growth and that's also how the company can benefit and can keep growing. For example, after Joyce took over Torrey Hills sales, she became very good at communicating with customers and solving their issues. After a while, it was clear that she could sell. She felt comfortable dealing with people, and liked the job.

> *Another important team building point is to motivate people by reducing their workload. That may sound counter-intuitive, but it works for us. In our company, when you are extremely experienced and good at a certain task, it's time to move on, to delegate and seek out your next higher-level challenges.*

But then Ken came to her and said; "Now it's time to delegate. You should choose somebody to sell and get yourself out of sales, move up to a higher level, and see what else can be done to get more inquiries. You can do more than just to talk to people who seek you out; you should come up with ideas on how to get more inquiries, and how to develop a distribution network to greatly improve our sales."

So she delegated, handing over the sales job to another person and picking up on her previous marketing work, while also mentoring the new salesperson. She discovered that she was, in fact, now thinking at a higher level, working on how to find distributors, and how best to work with representatives and distributors to explore a bigger market.

Our company keeps growing bigger and stronger because of this policy, and the challenge of moving up to higher level work ensures that the employees also keep growing, not getting stale doing repetitive work. That's how we became an Inc. 5000 company; those are the companies that have achieved the most growth, and for five consecutive years we've made that list.

Last, but not least, is to reward employees for their achievements in multiple ways. First, of course, is the pay raise. Even in the most difficult economic times, back in early 2000, we always got a little raise very year. At first, it was 5 percent. When the economy was down, we still got 2 percent. It made employees feel valued because their hard work was clearly appreciated and still got rewarded. And it's important to give people promotions. Even if their job function hasn't changed much, it's important to recognize their work and promote them to a higher level. Whenever we get a promotion, we feel obliged to work even harder and smarter to prove our value to the company.

Reward employees for their achievements in multiple ways.

While pay raises are part of the story, our company also has a policy of nominating employees for awards. That provides more of a spiritual boost that works to build your confidence and your sense of achievement. Ken is very good about nominating employees for awards that extol their value in the community or among their peers. Even when you don't win the award, simply being

Our company also has a policy of nominating employees for awards.

at the ceremony among other high achievers makes you feel like a winner.

Teambuilding means giving everyone on the team a reason to feel good about being a part of your shared successes; the strength to face their own mistakes and challenges and rise above them; and the opportunity to grow and take the company with them. Look at what you're doing to build your winning team, and see how you can "up your game."

MCMASTER ISSUES; HOW WE SUBCONSCIOUSLY TRY TO AVOID SOLVING TOUGH PROBLEMS

Did you ever find yourself using a work-around to avoid dealing with a knotty problem, even though that work-around might be unsatisfactory or even more work than digging in and solving the problem would be?

You may be familiar with the company McMaster-Carr, which is a big online distributor for industrial products. If someone needs some small parts, like screws, or different drill bits, everybody in the industry will typically go to McMaster to buy them.

McMaster had some problems with the US government some years back, related to their having inadvertently shipped some parts to a foreign country that was on a "do not sell to" list, and thus breaking the export laws. They were fined for that, and subsequently were more careful about exporting their parts. Our company, as you know, does some of its manufacturing in Mainland China. Ken went to McMaster-Carr to buy some drill bits, and when they asked, "How are you going to use this?"

Ken replied, "I'm going to send this to the factory in China." When they heard that, they refused to sell to him. It was a simple component, so he was able to purchase it from someone else. But because of this interaction, somehow McMaster put Torrey Hills on their "do not sell to" list.

A few years later, we won a major research and development grant from National Science Foundation. This was to be a US government-funded project that was to be completed here in San Diego. We needed to buy more components from McMaster. We contacted them, and to our surprise, were told that that they would not do business with us.

Now, that put us in a difficult position. As it happens, our company's headquarters has two suites in its building, and some years before Ken had subleased the second suite to a friend's company. We weren't going to be exporting these things, and it was for a government contract, so it seemed absurd that we had to deal with this issue. Ken's friend in the other suite suggested that he could order the parts, and have them shipped to his company next door, and circumvent the ban that way. But after considering it, Ken decided not to do it. For him, it just didn't pass the "sniff test"; it felt underhanded and not quite right.

He realized that what he was trying to do was to bypass the big challenge, which was to convince McMaster that they should take Torrey Hills off the "do not sell to" list and let Torrey Hills order components from them. We are a legitimate business, yet here we were, thinking about ways to get past their gatekeepers. We pulled together all kinds of documentation to make our case with McMaster to demonstrate that we were legitimate; we promised we'd never export to other countries without authorization, and we were in commercial business. It took a while to change their minds, but we did it. The lesson learned from this was that we have a tendency, if the problem seems too hard to solve, to waste time and energy looking for an easy way around it, rather than taking the harder road to a real solution.

Another example of this kind of thinking happened when Ken went to visit a customer in China. This customer was using our copper tungsten heat sink, which is one of the products we make. Ken has been working in the industry for 20 years, so of course has a lot of expertise by virtue of that experience. But in the meeting, he was surprised when one of the engineers asked him, "How do you clean the vacuum grease off the parts?" Ken explained that there were many ways to do it: using degreasing, using soap, using alkaline cleaning, all kinds of cleaning methods, etc., but Ken also asked, "Why are you trying to clean the parts?" He couldn't understand why they needed to clean it on the massive scale they'd described. When he pressed them to explain why the equipment needed so much cleaning, they mentioned that some of their parts had leaking issues and had to be screened 100 percent using vacuum-leak testing.

> *We have a tendency, if the problem seems too hard to solve, to waste time and energy looking for an easy way around it, rather than taking the harder road to a real solution.*

Ken realized at that point that they were trying to avoid addressing the real problem, which was the leak. When you make an electronic part, it sometimes needs to be hermetically sealed. It will have to be inspected periodically, but in fact, if you've done a good job with that initial seal, you should only have to run a few tests to make sure that it's still 100 percent hermetic. But instead of solving the problem directly, this customer had decided to inspect 100 percent to screen a hermeticity issue. Why? Because fixing that leak might be more challenging than inspecting 100 percent. Instead, they were opting to solve the easier problem.

Anyone in a technological industry knows that making a perfect part is difficult. Instead of trying to solve the problem that's creating the defects, most companies are going to say, "Okay, we're just going to make more parts, and hire additional people to sort them out." This is bad, because you're building in a lot of unnecessary costs into your production. Even when it's difficult, short-term or work-around solutions like this just aren't good enough. As a business, you have to face the tough things and go at them directly. Sometimes, we sub-consciously choose to ignore the bigger challenge and seek the easy way out. This is true for many small start-up companies; if we face a big issue, then we may decide to simply change direction. And the whole team will feel good about it—"Hey, let's do it this way for now, and we can deal with that other thing on the back end."

> **As a business, you have to face the tough things and go at them directly.**

We do it all the time. In manufacturing, at home, even in government; sometimes it's just easier to punt, and leave the big messy thing for the next guy to clean up.

Look at the immigration issues this country is wrestling with. Congress after Congress has opted to simply kick the can down the road, and leave the problem to be solved by the next generation. The list of things that government talks about and fails to act upon is long. We as business people can't afford to be quite so ready to look away, however. To survive, as a leader, you have to be fully conscious of what direction you're choosing to take, and why.

If you find yourself changing direction, it's important to listen to that little voice you hear telling you that while it may feel like a good idea, you're really just trying to avoid confrontation with a big challenge.

> *To survive, as a leader, you have to be fully conscious of what direction you're choosing to take, and why.*

We often see this kind of thing crop up in the Human Resources department. If somebody has performance-related issues, often managers try to avoid discussing the problem. Nobody wants to be the bad guy, nobody really wants to place blame or make an enemy. Because of this, you'll see sub-par performers getting shifted around in a company again and again, and not necessarily into a position in which they'll be able to make a contribution, because HR and everyone else are just hoping that one day their performance will improve without anyone having to confront the person and his or her issues directly.

Managers, that just doesn't work; not for the company, not for the employee. Bite the bullet and have that honest, face-to-face meeting. It can be uncomfortable, but you have to do it.

We had a customer in Boston about four years ago who was buying a lot of copper tungsten from us. Then, one day, the customer doubled the volume. We had another customer in San Diego at the same time that had doubled their volume, too. All of a sudden, our manufacturing volume more than doubled in a short period of time, and we found ourselves with troublesome production issues. It took a long time for us to iron out the problems, and finally, the Boston customer was so mad at us that he said his company would never do business with us again. Naturally, this was tremendously frustrating, and we felt terrible. This had been a great customer for us, and we liked and highly respected the company's owner, a man in his early 70s. But we parted, with hard feelings on his side, much to our regret—especially for Ken, who'd had a great relationship with this gentleman before the problems.

As it happened, last year Ken attended a big technical conference in Seattle. At the conference, a number of companies had big exhibits set up—and one of the companies exhibiting was this same Boston company from whom we'd parted so unhappily. Ken was walking around the exhibition area when he spotted the company's exhibit, and saw the gentleman there. He was about 50 yards away, and he hadn't seen Ken. Impulsively, Ken turned away, and headed down another aisle to avoid him. Then, he stopped; he knew that he was avoiding the man because he didn't want to be seen and to be thrust into an awkward situation—and that reaction just didn't cut it. Squaring his shoulders, Ken reversed direction and went directly up to the exhibition booth, straight toward the man he'd been ready to avoid.

He walked up to him and said, "It's been a while since the last time we spoke. I know you are really mad at me. I'm sorry. I just wanted to come by to say hi." To Ken's surprise and relief, the man responded warmly, extending his hand and saying that he understood what Ken had gone through, adding, "Sometimes life is a lot easier if you can control the rate of company business growth. Ten or fifteen percent, you should be happy—but if you suddenly shoot up by double, it will screw you up." The expected confrontation that Ken had been ready to avoid turned into a really pleasant conversation. If he'd let his fear make the choice for him, this would never have happened.

Like a lot of people, Ken has a deep-seated fear of speaking to groups of people, but he's often the organizer of conferences and as the General Chair he's required to address the attendees. He's shared that fact with a lot of the people who have seen him speak, and they always express amazement, even disbelief, because his nerves never seem to show. But it's a real challenge for him—his hands literally perspire as he's waiting for his name to be announced. And he stays nervous—right up until the moment that his name is called and he rises to speak. Once he stands up, somehow all his nerves fall away and he's completely calm. Again, it's the fear of facing the problem that holds us back, or makes us turn away to look for a way around it. Yet, if we dare to approach it directly, so often, the problem shrinks the closer we get to it.

The fact is, when confronting a big issue, a lot of the fear we have is imaginary. We think, "It's going to be so difficult—I'd better take another way." Don't give in to your fears of the unknown; face the challenges head-on. You'll find the satisfaction

> *If he'd let his fear make the choice for him, this would never have happened.*

you get from dealing with them conclusively is a much better reward than the momentary relief you may feel at having dodged them temporarily. Avoidance is a bad habit you can break.

Avoidance is a bad habit you can break.

WRITING WINNING PROPOSALS

This topic actually springs from a talk that Ken had with a good friend of his, a gentleman with a PhD in physics from UCSD. They were discussing research opportunities, and the friend said, "I have so many good ideas, but it's very hard for me to get any grants for research funding in order to work on them. What am I doing wrong?" This is a smart fellow, certainly someone whose ideas deserved financial support. Why couldn't he get it?

The first thing that popped up in Ken's mind was a famous quote from President John F. Kennedy: "Ask not what your country can do for you, but what you can do for your country." Ken repeated it to his friend, who looked back at him in puzzlement.

"Okay, I know the speech," he said. "What are you trying to tell me?"

Ken answered, "Here's what I'm trying to tell you. You have a lot of great ideas."

"Yeah."

"And you ask somebody to help you realize those ideas, but for some reason, it isn't happening. So why does nobody do it?

Basically, it's because you always ask the country what it can do for you, rather than looking at it from the other perspective. What problems are you trying to solve for investors?"

This kind of "me-first" thinking is typical for a lot of small business start-ups and the engineers and scientists who head them. It sounds harsh to put it this way, but it's true; most people are self-centered.

To give another example, when Ken had his first grant, he was trying to hire his first PhD. An assistant professor from Syracuse University called, a guy with a great background who wanted to join our company. Here's how Ken summarizes the man's pitch: "I am so good. I have so many great ideas, and I have many publications. If you give me a chance, in a few years, when I finish working out all my great ideas, I may even win a Nobel Prize." Very impressive, in its way, but it failed to answer the basic underlying question in any job interview, which is the employer's question, "What's in it for me?" As a business, we are not in the business of setting him up to win a Nobel Prize. We're not in the business of helping him get very famous. It's simply not within our sphere of interest. It's not why we hire people. Our interests dictate that we find the right person to help us get our project done, get it commercialized, and make it successful. Our first interest is the company's success, not his.

His mistake was really asking Ken what Ken could do for him. He never answered fundamental question: "If you join our company, what can you do for us?"

Ken participates in a kind of idea-sharing group with other engineers, who meet together to discuss things they're interested in working on, which creates an opportunity to workshop intellectual notions with like-minded people who understand the subject. He meets weekly with an advisor, and is himself an advisor to another engineer. At various times, he's gone into his meeting full of great ideas for products and innovations. At one of these meetings, his advisor, Dr. Sam Lee, heard him out, and then joked, "You have a solution, but you're waiting for problems."

Ken said, "What do you mean?"

Dr. Lee answered, "You have a lot of great ideas. You have a solution—but where's the problem?" And he was right—because in order to justify the thing Ken wanted to do, someone would have to be on the other end who needed it enough to pay for it, and Ken had no notion at that point who that future customer would be.

Here's a good rule of thumb: If you are trying to solve a problem, but nobody's willing to pay for you to do so, then that is not a real problem. It's an imaginary problem, because as a business, you've got to solve a problem someone is willing to pay to have solved. To put it in four simple words, "Show me the money." In our experience, if you can't do that, you'd better turn your attention to something more meaningful, and more profitable. Have you heard the saying, "If you give a two-year-old a hammer, the whole

> *If you are trying to solve a problem, but nobody's willing to pay for you to do so, then that is not a real problem. It's an imaginary problem, because as a business, you've got to solve a problem someone is willing to pay to have solved.*

world becomes a nail?" If you just have one solution in hand, you're going to waste a lot of energy and effort trying to find a problem it solves.

Dr. Lee's remark made Ken laugh, but it stung a little too, as he realized the truth of what he'd said. So often we have a solution, but we're still waiting for a problem. Make sure you see the customer's order before you start wasting work and money on a solution nobody may want.

Go talk to your customer. He's the one who'll buy it, if it's what he needs. But maybe, in the course of your talk, you'll discover that he wants something different—and that's what you should be working on. Let all your genius, your art, and your product department efforts come from the customer. Don't go to him with a pitch; listen to his problems, and turn your mind to solving them, if you want to succeed.

When Ken was talking to his friend who'd been frustrated in his search for research and development money, he tried to explain how to apply this to his own work. A few weeks prior to their conversation, the Boston Marathon bombing had killed three people and injured many more. A week prior to that, a New York City ferry had plowed into the dock because nobody in the crew had been paying attention, and several people were injured. Ken's friend's expertise was in lasers.

Ken asked him what his approach to the investors had been. Basically, it boiled down to, "I have a vision, and I need your money to make it happen." Ken suggested that, instead, his message should be, "I have a capability. Here's a problem, and here's what I can do to solve it." What about a proposal for a laser system that could remotely detect explosives? Consider those two terrorist brothers in Boston; because they had handled a lot of explosives, they'd be covered in explosive molecules from the TNT, although it would be in a low concentration. When you go through airport security, they have trained dogs checking the luggage for any kind of contraband: drugs, explosives, even fruit or meat. Your bad-guy bomber who's packing TNT will have a sort of halo around him of TNT molecules. The naked eye will not see it, but maybe with the right instrumentation, it can be detected.

Ken said, "Can you use your laser detection technology to solve this problem?" Ken's friend's eyes were opened. We're not sure if he ever wrote a subsequent proposal, but he knew what Ken was saying. Ken had another suggestion too: "Can you use your laser detection to prevent the next ferry crash?" That's not a far-fetched idea by any means; automotive technology already exists for collision avoidance and is available in some of the high-end cars. If you get too close to somebody, or to an object, the radar can tell you, "Hey, you are too close to the big semi in front of you." The radar will apply the brake before you can even react, to slow you down a little. A similar technology could be used to create an automated warning system for a ferry, one that would tell the captain to slow the boat's thrust or even to reverse it to avoid colliding with the dock.

> *Again, we're talking about real-life problems that need real-life solutions, not pie in the sky.*

Again, we're talking about real-life problems that need real-life solutions, not pie in the sky.

FROM START-UP TO STAR

Over the years, we have received a lot of research and development grants from the government, both on the US side and the China side. We've received multiple grants from the government of China. As for the US side, we received two grants from California for the EIASG, and we also received several grants from the National Science Foundation. We got them because, basically, we follow the solid scientific principle of trying to solve a problem, not to ask government to give us money because we have a particular exciting technology. And we're very clear about that in our presentations to them when we make our applications: "We have a solution to solve a real-life problem."

It was Zig Ziglar who famously said, "You can have everything in life you want, if you will just help enough other people get what they want." Don't be self-centered, because you can't expect others to feel the same way about you. Basically, as a business, if you want to get something, always make sure others get what they want first.

> **"You can have everything in life you want, if you will just help enough other people get what they want."**

This kind of cart-before-the-horse thinking can backfire in all kinds of arenas. It's very common in job interviews, for instance, to walk in talking about what you are looking for, or what you hope to get out of a job: "Oh, I want to make $70,000 a year." Instead, in the interview, your attitude should be, "Okay, what are your company's needs, and how can I help you to meet those needs?"

That's what your interviewer is interested in, and it's what you should be interested in, too.

When we're doing sales or writing proposals, we often have a tendency to concentrate on what we know we want. "I have exciting technology. I just need the money from you so I can realize my goal." But if I go in with that attitude, why would somebody fund me?

So how do you write a winning proposal? Make sure that you've made the effort to identify other people's needs, to try to solve a real problem, and then present a solution. Approached in this way, the chance of getting a proposal approved, whether it's a sales proposal or a research proposal, is a lot higher than it will be if you go in with, "Give me this funding, and I'll be successful and famous," as your pitch. Charles Karrass said it well: "In business, as in life, you don't get what you deserve. You get what you negotiate."

How do you write a winning proposal? Make sure that you've made the effort to identify other people's needs, to try to solve a real problem, and then present a solution.

—

"In business, as in life, you don't get what you deserve. You get what you negotiate."

Governments have to be especially sensitive to how you pitch your proposal. How exactly is what you're proposing going to improve the lives of the taxpayers who will be funding it? No matter how brilliant you are, they're not really interested in making you famous. Scientists and engineers love the process of innovation for its own sake, and most people are so focused in the excitement of the ideas and the data that they forgot to answer the question of why this is important to the taxpayer. It's common to see proposals written for research and development money that spend more than half of their page space focusing on why this research is so exciting, and how it will improve the available data, instead of honing in on why it should matter to whoever's paying the tab for it, or whether the problem is of sufficient significance to matter to the taxpayer. Henry Kaiser, who did pretty well for himself, when asked the secret of success, said, "Find a need, and fill it."

If you're approaching a venture capitalist with a proposal that's just a variation on the theme, "I have a solution waiting for a problem," that proposal is going to the bottom of the pile—or into the "circular file." A good portion of any business plan should explain clearly why this is a problem, present a thorough analysis of it, then address why the problem deserves solutions and who would be willing to pay. If you can get those questions answered up front, your chances are far greater that he will continue to read to find out what your solution is—and will give you the funding you're seeking.

"Find a need, and fill it."

WE GET MORE BY ASKING FOR LESS

A re you familiar with Robert Cialdini's Six Principles of Influence? You should be. One of them is called *reciprocity*. As humans, we generally aim to return favors, pay back debts, and treat others as they treat us. According to the idea of reciprocity, we should do something nice, something of value to another person or company first, especially when they may be of help to us in the future. When the time comes, they will be more likely to return the favor or do business with us because they feel indebted to us and obliged to offer their help.

Here are some examples. We have had all kinds of customers during our years of operations. Some are Fortune 500 companies, while others are small to medium-size companies that have achieved great things. One of the things we have done consistently to support them is to nominate successful customers

> *As humans, we generally aim to return favors, pay back debts, and treat others as they treat us.*

to receive awards, such as "Best Innovation" awards, or best new product awards, so that they can be recognized. First, we write them an e-mail asking for their permission to submit a nomination, and then we prepare the nomination material to the best of our abilities, and hope for the best outcome for the company. Sometimes, we've succeeded and we at least got them into the finalist list; sometimes not, but all the customers nominated appreciated our initiative and became our customers for life.

We also write support letters. For example, we have a new salesman who received an e-mail when he was following up with a customer, who said, "I'm working on a research proposal on size reduction of biomass. It would make the proposal much stronger if we could have a supportive letter from your company. It would generate great cooperation between us if that proposal is success-fully funded." This customer was a professor who was trying to get funding. He didn't have the money yet to buy from us, because his project was still in the proposal stage, which suggested to the young salesman that it was perhaps a long shot as far as a sale was concerned.

This new salesman went to Ken and asked him whether we should take the time and write a support letter for the customer. Ken

> *Ken has made a lot of friends by providing grant writing support letters, and making friends is very important, because whenever they have a need in the future, they will come to you for a solution.*

replied that this is a classic story of cost and value; the cost of time. We don't have to write the support letter, but over the years, Ken has made a lot of friends by providing grant writing support letters, and making friends is very important, because whenever they have a need in the future, they will come to you for a solution. That's why it was important for the sales rep to work with this customer, to write that letter and to make the professor a friend of ours.

A typical support letter goes like this: "Torrey Hills Technologies is pleased to support this company on [the proposed project]. Torrey Hills is a leader in developing quality, yet affordable, heat sinks for high-tech electronics and electronic packaging. We are very interested in cooperating with this company to develop their technology. We are anticipating great potential in application in the proposed heat sink. Once the proposed heat sink is proven to be feasible, we would like to cooperate with this company for future commercialization, utilizing our well-established marketing channels." Although it's hard to say whether this professor could get this grant to have money to make a purchase from us, it was still important to cooperate with him, make a friend, and probably turn him into a customer in the future.

For heat sinks, sometimes if the customer has no immediate need, it helps to help the customer do their business first. We supply heat sinks to our customers so that they can make packages and other electronic devices to supply to their customers. Because of our extensive industry reach and our established industry network, we can spot new business opportunities for their business, introducing them to potential buyers and making their business stronger. Our idea is that as long as they have strong growth, we are going to be likely to sell more components to them to support their growth. They'll be loyal to us in the meantime, because we can be so much more valuable than other suppliers in the market. Through helping the customer build their business, we eventually get more business from this customer.

Torrey Hills Copper Tungsten (CuW) and
Copper Molybdenum (CuMo) Heat Sinks

Next is *give first and give graciously*. The simplest form of what we give is something for free. Free offerings are a very useful tool to attract new clients and reward customer loyalty; for example, free samples. We have small packages of samples that we distribute to potential buyers to prove the quality and reliability of our product before they make the commitment to buy from us. For equipment, we offer free trials and demonstrations. They can send their materials over to our office and we

Next is give first and give graciously.

process the material to prove to them that the machine will work for their application.

We have a team of expert engineers in our company who can give free professional advice to our customers on what machine they should use, or what kind of rollers they should use, as well as what speed they should use while processing their material. For existing clients, we can provide special volume discounts. If they keep buying from us, we will offer very generous discounts to keep them as loyal customers.

Besides these ways of giving, we also give more complicated value. For example, when our T65 model three roll mill was first out, we offered this trade-in program; if the customer traded in their used mill, no matter what the condition of it was or even if their three roll mill was made by our biggest competitor, we would give them a credit of $3,000 toward purchasing a new machine made by our company. This demonstrated to them the confidence that we have in our brand. We stand behind our equipment 100 percent and we offer an incredible value in order for them to try out our machine.

For our furnace product, we have a partner in China who is our supplier. Their 20th anniversary was coming up, and we were thinking about what kind of gift we should send them. We decided on a specially engraved crystal award. On it, we had inscribed "Happy 20th Anniversary," of course, along with all the logos of the many, many companies that we have sold their furnaces to, because this success has been a joint effort. It's an incredible piece, very beautiful, and the logos make it quite impressive. It's a great recognition of the work they have done. We made a point, too, to send two engineers to their manufacturing facility to attend their events on the day of the anniversary. When they presented the award, it was a huge boost to our relationship with the supplier.

We also give out a lot of gift baskets. This is more about giving graciously, to appreciate customers or someone who has done us a great favor. For great customers, we sent out gift baskets around Christmas time or before the holidays; also for people who have offered us help, such as referring new customers or writing recommendations for us. These acts of recognition and thanks all help us to build great relationships with our partners.

The next point is to be sure that your customer always gets more than they pay for. This is especially true when you're dealing with smaller companies. At big companies, they evaluate their purchasing options and issue a purchase order soon afterward. But for smaller companies, they're likely to debate quite a bit over whether it is wise to make that investment. To help them reach a decision, we have to make sure we always

> *This is more about giving graciously, to appreciate customers or someone who has done us a great favor.*

offer more value than they pay for. Sometimes, it's not the actual cost of the product, but the perceived value in their mind that makes the difference.

For example, some customers have a certain budget within which they have to work, and they may be debating between a used piece of equipment and our brand-new equipment. That's a typical case of cost versus value. For used equipment, they pay considerably less, so how do we justify them making a bigger investment and buying our new product?

We explain to them that used equipment typically does not come with a warranty. Sometimes there isn't even a manual, so if anything goes wrong, there is nobody to support them or to help them fix their machine. Sometimes, if the machine is 10 or 20 years old, spare parts may no longer be available to help the machine work again. We tell them that the value here is, if you pay more to get the brand-new machine, you have our service 24/7. If something goes wrong, we ship you spare parts overnight to keep your production running. Our extended warranty means you don't have to worry about spare parts, and you don't have to worry about customer service. We are always there to support you. Most customers evaluate these two options and then decide to purchase a new machine from us because in their perceived value system, customer service counts for a lot.

> *Most customers evaluate these two options and then decide to purchase a new machine from us because in their perceived value system, customer service counts for a lot.*

Sometimes, for a certain purchase price, customers are reluctant to move ahead. They need something more. They need more value in the purchasing price to persuade themselves that this is a good deal. So, instead of reducing the price, we will sometimes extend the warranty. Instead of a one-year warranty, we make it two to three years so they don't have to worry about the machine breaking down, because we stand behind our product. We're confident that the machine won't have any big problems within three years, so for us, it costs nothing or it costs very little. We probably just make a trip to the customers if something goes wrong, but for the customer, it's a great value because it guarantees worry-free operation for three years.

Sometimes, we will throw in a lot of spare parts that they are likely to need over the years. For example, they will need to replace the end plate, they need to replace the blade; that's normal wear and tear, and they would otherwise have to pay for these spare parts in the years to come. At the time of purchase, we include these spare parts for free for three years, and in their minds, the perceived value is very high relative to our actual cost, so they are happy to move ahead and to issue a purchase order to us.

It's always a good idea to make sure that your collaborators walk away with more than you do. We pay a lot of attention to distributors. They're a big part of our sales network. We offer a 30 percent discount to our distributors. That does not leave a lot of profit for our own company, but we believe a good profit margin is important to encourage the distributors to do a good job and actively seek out customers. Having a good distributor is very important; they have their own network, and they have their own industry connections to reach out to specific customers. If they don't work

> *It's always a good idea to make sure that your collaborators walk away with more than you do. We pay a lot of attention to distributors.*

hard for us, then we can't grow out our market further, so we're willing to offer them a 30 percent discount on products in order to reward their hard work with our company and to make them think that we are a generous and trustworthy long-term partner.

For example, this firm has a partner in China. We were talking with IBM for an order, and we were really eager to get them as a customer, no matter what it would take, because IBM is a big-name brand and it would enhance our marketplace credibility if they agreed to try out our product. In order to secure it, we gave them a huge discount, but not at the sacrifice of our partner. We can't just tell our partner, "Because this is a famous customer, can you please reduce the price significantly so that we can get their business?" We actually took on this loss ourselves. We still got the machine from them at pretty much the regular selling price, and then we distributed the furnace to IBM. We took a loss, but we ended up winning this customer, making us credible in the market. The idea behind the strategy was to get more customers in the future, to guarantee that we get good business and good profits from future customers, but it wouldn't have been right or fair to sacrifice suppliers' interests in order to help ourselves gain more market credibility.

Some companies assume they will do better by selling something directly, cutting out the middleman, but this is not so. Our Korean market is a good example of why that's a bad idea. We got a lot of inquiries from Korea, but we never sold anything to that market, because it's a protected market and they rely on the distributors in their own countries. Thus, we ended up working with a distributor in Korea. We offered him a 30 percent discount on our own machines, and he has done a great job, selling one to two units per month at the start with the volume quickly increasing. That's why it's critical to get a local distributor instead of trying to sell the product yourself in a particular region, in order to get a bigger profit.

In China, also, we have an exclusive distributor. They are the experts in the area, and we offer a very high discount to them. They had this selling operation system in which they would go out and find second-tier distributors all over the country, because they are more familiar with the local markets. Because we offer them a big profit margin, they have the resources to give their second-tier distributors a good percentage of commissions to expand the market.

Likewise, in Latin America, we have distributors that work well for us because they speak the local language. One of them got a constant stream of business for us just because of his connections in Latin America and because of his language skills. When you include your sales team distributors and the middleman in profits, even though you may get less for a sale, you will make more sales, especially so when you're trying hard to expand your market share. When you introduce something new to the market, and not a lot of people know about this product, it is important to be ready to sacrifice your own profits to get more people to sell your product. That way, you gain the momentum to get more customers to try out your product. We need volume to reduce cost. We need more satisfied customers out there to establish credibility for the brand, so it really helps.

This is why we say that maximum value can be achieved through joint efforts. More products will be

> *Maximum value can be achieved through joint efforts.*

sold, plus the sales team, distributor, and middleman get rewarded for their networks and their efforts. Customers always perceive that they're getting more than they paid for, so they're happy too. Everyone ends up being a winner.

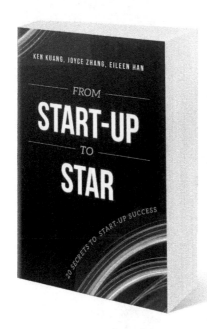

How can you use this book?

MOTIVATE

EDUCATE

THANK

INSPIRE

PROMOTE

CONNECT

Why have a custom version of *From Start-Up to Star*?

- Build personal bonds with customers, prospects, employees, donors, and key constituencies

- Develop a long-lasting reminder of your event, milestone, or celebration

- Provide a keepsake that inspires change in behavior and change in lives

- Deliver the ultimate "thank you" gift that remains on coffee tables and bookshelves

- Generate the "wow" factor

Books are thoughtful gifts that provide a genuine sentiment that other promotional items cannot express. They promote employee discussions and interaction, reinforce an event's meaning or location, and they make a lasting impression. Use your book to say "Thank You" and show people that you care.

Printed in the USA
CPSIA information can be obtained
at www.ICGtesting.com
JSHW012053140824
68134JS00035B/3410